Outcome-Based Education:

Critical Issues and Answers

By William G. Spady

The American Association of School Administrators

Library of Congress Catalog Card Number: 94-079574
ISBN: 0-87652-183-9
AASA Stock Number: 21-00488

This book was reviewed by AASA and approved for publication. Approval does not signify that
the contents reflect the views or policies of AASA.

Foreword
Comments from the Field

Ron Brandt
*Executive Editor,
Association for
Supervision and
Curriculum
Development*

American education needs this book. Because of massive technological, economic, and social changes, we are challenged to boost standards of student performance substantially, especially among those who in the past were least successful. The education sector apparently will not have more money, so we cannot expect salaries to be more attractive or other resources more plentiful. The alternative, say thoughtful observers, is to restructure.

Until recently, that seemed to be the consensus. National business leaders urged educators to follow their example in making their organizations more responsive and efficient. Governors offered to stop issuing mandates in exchange for "results." Although at the local level very little restructuring was actually going on, the major question facing educators was not whether it should be done, but how to do it.

William Spady has answers for that question. With a background in sociology, a brilliant mind, and an innovative spirit, Spady has spent much of his professional life refining those answers. His ideas are offered within a framework that, when stated in general terms, seems almost self-evident: Define what students are expected to learn and redesign the system to make sure they have maximum opportunity to learn it. Most professional educators are familiar with that general principle; it is inherent in a well-established formula for planning curricula made famous by Ralph Tyler — but its apparent simplicity is deceptive.

The fact is schools do not operate in accord with that commonsense principle. Yes, schools have goals and objectives, and teachers and principals work very hard — within existing constraints — to foster student learning. But in recent years, as educators and political leaders sought common ground and began to lay the foundation for an outcome-based system, it became clear that such a system is necessarily very different from the one we know so well.

Among those who recognized that a system truly based on outcomes requires modification of some conventional practices, such as tracking and competitive grading, were traditionalists who treasure these practices. They came to see Outcome-Based Education as the embodiment of all the modernist tendencies they most deplore in contemporary schooling. Educators sometimes added to those misgivings by listing as outcomes qualities they hoped children would acquire, such as positive self-esteem and global mindedness, which critics regarded as unattainable or undesirable. As a result, outcome-based education is now considered by many people, both educators and citizens, as highly suspect.

What has been lacking is a clear, thoughtful interpretation of what Outcome-Based Education really is, why it is needed, and how it operates. No one is better qualified than Bill Spady to offer such an analysis, and in this book he provides it. I find his discussion to be highly readable, coherent, and convincing. I think it should become a classic, because the issues Spady examines are unavoidable. If we really want all students to learn, we must redesign the system of schooling so that they will.

Robert L. Simonds

President, Citizens for Excellence in Education

One of the most important values cherished by Traditionalists, and by Traditionalist Christians in particular, is reverence for fairness and objectivity. Indeed, the admonition of the second wisest man to ever walk the face of the earth — King Solomon — rings as true today as it did over 3,000 years ago: "He who answers a matter before hearing the whole of it is a fool." And again, "The first person to state his case seemeth to be right — until another comes along and examines him." In this book, William Spady has explicitly addressed most of the questions raised by Traditionalist Christians across the United States. The reader may not agree with all of his answers; in fact, the reader may not agree with any of his answers. But for Traditionalist Christians who are interested in fairness and in truth, this book presents a rare opportunity to discover exactly what the chief proponent of Outcome-Based Education really says, not what his most vocal critics say he said. Whether you are an ardent proponent or a dedicated opponent of the perspectives asserted in his book, you will have a valuable asset to buttress your arguments: a factual and accurate presentation based on what William Spady actually says about Outcome-Based Education, not on how others interpret it.

Table of Contents

Foreword
Comments from the Field iii
    Ron Brandt
    Robert L. Simonds

Chapter 1
What Does Outcome-Based Education Really Mean? 1
Highlights:
    Who should have a voice in determining a state's or district's outcomes?
    What does it mean to base education on outcomes?
    Are there any examples of outcome-based models?
    How is being "outcome-based" different from what schools have always done?
    What are the key elements of a sound outcome-based approach?
    How do OBE's expanded opportunity and high expectations principles work?
    Can OBE's principles be applied in "right" and "wrong"
        ways in schools and districts?
Summary 24
Figures:
    1.1 Examples of Outcome-Based Models 4
    1.2 The OBE Pyramid 8
    1.3 OBE's "Power" Principles 10
    1.4 Clarity of Focus 11
    1.5 Five Key Dimensions of Opportunity 13
    1.6 Three Key Dimensions of High Expectations 17
    1.7 The "Golden Rules" of Outcome-Based Curriculum Design 19
    1.8 An Outcome-Based Systems Framework 23

Chapter 2
Why Is There So Much Interest in Outcome-Based Reforms?   27

Highlights:

What are some of the key changes taking place in contemporary society and the economy that are directly shaping school reforms?

How is our Industrial Age educational system out of sync with today's Information Age trends and needs?

What key features of Industrial Age schools inherently constrain learning success for many students?

What are the outcome-based alternatives to these constraining paradigm components?

How do these OBE components relate to the Total Quality and Reengineering movements in American business?

What features of outcome-based models in daily life appeal so strongly to education reformers?

How does OBE provide parents and the public with more accurate and meaningful information about student learning and capabilities?

What do those implementing OBE find attractive about its cost and effectiveness?

Summary..48

Figures:

2.1 Components of the Time-Based, Industrial Age Paradigm 31

2.2. Components of the Outcome-Based, Information Age Paradigm..........36

2.3. Grades Are Accumulated Amalgamations 44

2.4. The Five Great Illusions of Achievement..45

Chapter 3
What Are Outcomes, and How Are They Derived? 49

Highlights:

What are outcomes?

What is the difference between an outcome and an "outcome of significance"?

Does the concept of culminating outcomes mean that everything learned before the end of a student's career doesn't matter?

Are specific content and skills important to those implementing OBE?

What goes into a demonstration of learning?

Do outcomes inevitably involve values and other affective factors?

How do role performances differ from what students were expected to do in the past?

Is it realistic for schools to prepare students to become successful at complex role performances?

How can schools define outcomes that will truly matter for
students beyond their schooling experience?

Summary...76
Figures:
    3.1 Avoid "Outcome Aliases"...50
    3.2 The Learning Performance Pyramid..................................54
    3.3 Two Paradigms of Learning 58
    3.4 Three Critical Domains of Outcomes.................................60
    3.5 The Demonstration Mountain..62
    3.6 Fundamental Life Performance Roles.................................69

Chapter 4
What Are the Major Trends in Outcome-Based Implementation?....79

Highlights:

What are the key configurations of OBE in today's school reform efforts?

What are the key characteristics of classroom reform, program
alignment, external accountability, and system transformation
approaches associated with OBE?

Can the term "OBE" be applied to all four of these approaches?

Can districts evolve from a Classroom Reform to a System
Transformation model?

Is it possible for individual schools to be outcome-based without
involving the total district?

Are there recognized standards for OBE implementation?

Summary...105
Figures:
    4.1 Face 1 OBE: Classroom Reform...82
    4.2 Face 2 OBE: Program Alignment.......................................85
    4.3 Face 3 OBE: External Accountability.................................89
    4.4 Face 4 OBE: System Transformation 95

Chapter 5
How Does Outcome-Based Implementation Affect
Schools and Students?..107

Highlights:

Are there any ideal models that schools should emulate?

Why does comprehensive implementation take so long?

What are some of the districts currently serving as models for others?

How has OBE affected the schools or students of actual districts involved
in implementing OBE?

How has OBE affected the staff and students of actual schools?

Summary...139

Chapter 6
Why All the Controversy About OBE?..............................141
Highlights:
    Who are the groups that have taken a stance against outcome-based reforms?
    Are these groups united in their opposition?
    What do these groups and critics hope to accomplish by derailing OBE?
    What about outcome-based reforms do these organized
        groups find objectionable?
    Should parents, taxpayers, policymakers, and educators be
        concerned about these issues?
    What are the controversies surrounding the questions of governmental
        control, philosophy and "world view," and what outcomes are?
    What are the controversies surrounding what's proven versus experimental,
        and the question of instructional opportunities?
    What groups have actively supported outcome-based reforms?
    What do these groups hope to gain through OBE implementation?
    What other major school reform initiatives are closely allied with OBE?
    Are the controversies over these reforms reconcilable?

Summary...170
Figures
    6.1 Understanding OBE reforms..154
    6.2 The Fixed Commodity Paradigm of Achievement........................163
    6.3 The Expandable Commodity Paradigm of Achievement...................164

Chapter 7
Where Does OBE Go From Here? 173
Highlights:
    What is the short-term future of OBE?
    What is the most optimistic scenario of the future of
        outcome-based reforms? What is the least optimistic?
    What is the most probable scenario?
    What can those who support outcome-based reforms do to keep them
        alive in their districts and states?

Conclusion...187
Glossary...189
Bibliography...195
OBE Implementation Resources...197
Background Reading on OBE..199
Acknowledgments..203
About the Author...207

Chapter 1
What Does Outcome-Based Education Really Mean?

This opening chapter addresses a range of issues related to the meaning of the term Outcome-Based Education (OBE). It provides definitions of key terms and concepts and describes the foundations and examples of genuine outcome-based models. These definitions and examples are the grounding for everything else in this book.

1. What does the term "Outcome-Based Education" really mean?

Outcome-Based Education means clearly focusing and organizing everything in an educational system around what is essential for all students to be able to do successfully at the end of their learning experiences. This means starting with a clear picture of what is important for students to be able to do, then organizing curriculum, instruction, and assessment to make sure this learning ultimately happens. The keys to having an outcome-based system are:

　　1) Developing a clear set of learning outcomes around which
　　　all of the system's components can be focused.

2) Establishing the conditions and opportunities within the system that enable and encourage all students to achieve those essential outcomes.

2. What exactly are outcomes?

Outcomes are clear learning results that we want students to demonstrate at the end of significant learning experiences. They are not values, beliefs, attitudes, or psychological states of mind. Instead, outcomes are what learners can actually do with what they know and have learned — they are the tangible application of what has been learned. This means that outcomes are actions and performances that embody and reflect learner competence in using content, information, ideas, and tools successfully. Having learners do important things with what they know is a major step beyond knowing itself.

Because outcomes involve actual doing, rather than just knowing or a variety of other purely mental processes, they must be defined according to the actions or demonstration processes being sought. When defining and developing outcomes, educators must use observable action verbs — like describe, explain, design, or produce — rather than vague or hidden nondemonstration processes — like know, understand, believe, and think.

For example, the possible outcome "explain the major causes of inflation in capitalist economies" implies that to be successful the learner will be expected to develop both the competence of explaining and the knowledge of the major causes of inflation in capitalist economies.

Since outcome-based systems expect learners to carry out the processes defined within an outcome statement, they are careful to build those processes directly into the outcome through demonstration verbs. Therefore, one key to recognizing a well-defined outcome is to look for the demonstration verb or verbs that define which processes the learner is expected to carry out at the end. Without those verbs, what are called outcome statements lack a clearly defined demonstration process, and without that defined process the outcome statement takes on the character of a goal rather than a true outcome demonstration.

Finally, because outcomes occur at or after the end of a learning experience, it is useful to think of them representing the ultimate result that is sought from the learning. When the notion of an ultimate result is applied to the end of the student's career in school, rather than to particular segments of curriculum or blocks of time, OBE often uses the term

"Exit Outcome." As we will see illustrated in Chapters 3 and 5, most exit outcomes are defined as broad performance capabilities, rather than as specific curriculum skills. This gives all of the district's students and staff an ultimate target toward which they can focus and orient their teaching and learning experiences. Specific curriculum knowledge and skills are developed from and around the exit outcomes and directly help students develop those broad performance abilities.

3. Who should have a voice in determining a state's or district's outcomes?

Historically, answers to this question have varied. (Chapter 3 explores this in greater depth.) However, the most advanced models of exit outcome design and development deliberately attempt to engage a community's key constituents and stakeholder groups. With the future of all students at stake, no one group should have the privilege or carry the responsibility for unilaterally determining this critical process.

4. What does it mean to base education on outcomes?

To base a system on something means defining, deciding, organizing, structuring, focusing, and operating what the system does according to some consistent standard or principle. In education, the calendar has been that unvarying standard or base throughout most of the 20th century. Virtually all components of the current system are defined, structured, and operated with time as the key determining factor. The nine-month school year has been the standard for how everything in the system is supposed to operate. Consequently, the most familiar way of operating schools is time-based.

Before basing a system on outcomes, states and districts must establish a clear framework of learning that students will be able to master successfully at the culminating point in their schooling careers — what was just referred to as exit outcomes. Then, districts must proceed to define, organize, structure, focus, and operate their activities based on those culminating outcomes.

A system based on outcomes gives top priority to ends, purposes, learning, accomplishments, and results. Decision making is consistent with these priorities. Often, an outcomes approach requires placing the system's traditional definers and shapers — time, procedures, programs, teaching, and curriculum — in a subordinate position. This essential shift from time to accomplishments often puts actual learning results on a collision course with the clock, schedule, and calendar. If time and accomplishments don't mesh, then the term "outcome-based" directly implies that outcomes must take precedence over time.

5. Are there any examples of outcome-based models?

The world is filled with examples of outcome-based models, and some of the more common ones are listed in Figure 1.1.

Outcome-based systems go back at least 500 years to the craft guilds of the Middle Ages in Europe. Over the centuries, these guilds evolved into various forms of apprenticeship training models, and they have been institutionalized as the way to design, deliver, and document instruction throughout today's business world.

Some contemporary examples of outcome-based models include technical training programs in the military, flight schools, ski schools, karate instruction, scuba instruction, and any other area of learning where clearly defined competence and performance are essential to carrying out a role effectively.

Other clear examples of performance credentialing are professional licensure of doctors, lawyers, real estate brokers, and cosmetologists, as well as merit and honor badges for Boy and Girl Scouts. Figure 1.1 also lists other examples familiar to millions of older Americans: one-room schoolhouses and parenting. Notice the only contemporary public schooling example is alternative high schools, but this picture is changing as more and more schools and districts initiate OBE efforts.

FIGURE 1.1

Examples of Outcome-Based Models

Craft Guilds of the Middle Ages
Apprenticeship Training in the
  Skilled Trades
Personnel Training in Business
Professional Licensure
Military Training Programs
Scouting Merit Badges
Karate Instruction
Scuba Instruction
Flight Schools
Ski Schools
One-Room Schoolhouses
"Alternative" High Schools
Parenting

While many of these examples differ considerably in terms of their operational features, they do share two key things. First, each model is focused on a clearly defined performance result for learners that is not compromised. Second, in each example WHAT and WHETHER students learn successfully is more important than WHEN and HOW they learn it. In short, as noted in the previous answer, successful learning results are more important to instructors in outcome-based models than the schedule they follow or the methods they use.

6. If outcome-based models are so prevalent outside of education, why don't more schools use them?

Part of this answer is historical. About a century ago, America's economy and society were in the midst of a profound change known today as the shift from the Agricultural Age to the Industrial Age. Large-scale immigration and urbanization accompanied this change. Public education also had to be expanded and institutionalized. The template for this new education system had many characteristics of the assembly-line factory — at the time considered the most advanced form of productive organization ever developed. Just as factories standardize their production processes around specific tasks at specific work stations on fixed schedules, schools have been compelled, often through law and accreditation procedures, to standardize their delivery systems.

The result of this standardization is the opposite of what outcome-based education promotes. In the Industrial Age model, WHEN and HOW students learn things too often take precedence over WHAT is learned and WHETHER it is learned well. In other words, the clock, schedule, calendar, and program characteristics are fixed, predefined, and unwavering. Yet, the definition and realization of student learning success are vague and highly variable.

However, some types of programs in the present system do focus on clear performance expectations for students, which they teach and assess accordingly. Vocational/technical, business, and performing arts programs are among them. But note that these programs lie outside what is usually considered the system's most important programs: its core academic curriculum. Academic programs have typically embodied very little of OBE's basic approaches to curriculum design, instructional delivery, and learning assessment.

7. How exactly is being "outcome-based" different from what schools have always done?

When lists of characteristics describe how traditional education systems differ from outcome-based systems, the main differences fall into four key areas:

- **Outcome-based systems build everything on a clearly defined framework of exit outcomes.** Curriculum, instructional strategies, assessments, and performance standards are developed and implemented to facilitate key outcomes. In OBE, curriculum, instruction, and assessment should be viewed as flexible and alterable means for accomplishing clearly defined learning "ends."

  In contrast, traditional systems already have a largely predefined curriculum structure with an assessment and credentialing system in place. They usually are not structured around clearly defined outcomes expected of all students. By and large, curriculum and assessment systems are treated as ends in themselves.

- **Time in an outcome-based system is used as an alterable resource, depending on the needs of teachers and students.** Within reasonable constraints, time is manipulated to the best advantage of all learners — some students learn some parts of the curriculum sooner, while others accomplish those parts later.

  In the traditional system, just the opposite is true. Time defines most system features; it is an inflexible constraint for teachers and students. The schedule and the calendar control student learning and success.

- **In an outcome-based system, standards are clearly defined, known, and "criterion-based" for all students.** As in the Girl and Boy Scouts, all students potentially are eligible to reach and receive full credit for achieving any performance standard in the system. There are no quotas on who can be successful or on what standards can be pursued.

  In contrast, the traditional system operates around a comparative/competitive approach to standards linked to a predetermined "curve" or quota of possible successes. Only some students are destined to do well, and only some get access to the most challenging areas of the curriculum. This process of sorting and selecting begins very early in the school years and evolves into an inflexible system of curriculum tracking by high school.

- **Outcome-based systems focus on increasing students' learning and ultimate performance abilities to the highest possible levels before they leave school.** In other words, OBE schools take a "macro" view of student learning and achievement. Mistakes are treated as inevitable steps along the way to having students develop, internalize, and demonstrate high-level performance capabilities. Working to continuously improve student learning before graduation, outcome-based systems define student achievement as the highest level of performance a student has been able to reach at any given point in time. Ultimate school achievement is directly reflected in what students can do successfully at or after their formal instructional experiences have ended.

> **Those who are slower never get the opportunity to truly catch up because their record of earlier mistakes cannot be erased.**

The current system takes quite the opposite approach, testing and permanently grading students every step of the way on all segments of the curriculum. All mistakes become part of a permanent record, which accumulates and constantly reminds students of past errors. The system emphasizes and rewards students for how well they do assigned work at the time it is initially covered in class. Those who are fast and consistent performers emerge with the best grades and records. Those who are slower never get the opportunity to truly catch up because their record of earlier mistakes cannot be erased.

But what is almost never assessed or documented is what either kind of student ultimately can do successfully to match this accumulation of grades.

8. What are the key elements of a sound outcome-based approach?

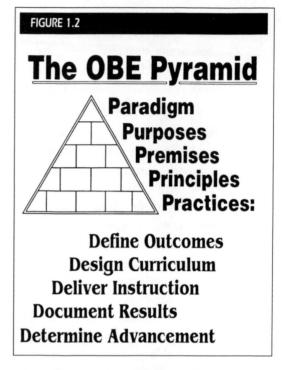

FIGURE 1.2

The OBE Pyramid

Paradigm
Purposes
Premises
Principles
Practices:

Define Outcomes
Design Curriculum
Deliver Instruction
Document Results
Determine Advancement

Sound outcome-based models incorporate several elements that work together to change how schools operate and facilitate learning success for students. These key elements are represented graphically in Figure 1.2 in what is called "The OBE Pyramid." Starting at the top, the Pyramid suggests the key OBE elements are: Paradigm of operating, two key Purposes, three key Premises, four operating Principles, and five generic domains of Practice. Each of these levels is described below.

9. What is the OBE paradigm?

Simply stated, a paradigm is a way of viewing and a way of doing things consistent with that viewpoint. As described earlier, the OBE paradigm that shapes decision making and patterns of concrete action is the viewpoint that WHAT and WHETHER students learn successfully is more important than WHEN and HOW they learn something. From a broader perspective, this orientation to schooling entails a fundamental shift in how the system operates — a shift that makes "accomplishing results" more important than simply "providing services." Implicit in the OBE paradigm is the desire to have all students emerge from the system as genuinely successful learners.

In more extended form, the paradigm is embodied in 10 characteristics shaping how schools or districts actually operate. These ten characteristics and the larger paradigm picture will be discussed in Chapter 2.

10. What are OBE's two purposes?

OBE's two key purposes reflect its underlying "Success for all students and staff" philosophy. They are:

- Ensuring that all students are equipped with the knowledge, competence, and qualities needed to be successful after they exit the educational system.

- Structuring and operating schools so that those outcomes can be achieved and maximized for all students.

In a nutshell, these two purposes commit the system to focus on the future performance abilities of students and to establish a success-oriented way of operating. They reject the prevalent notion that students of differing aptitudes or abilities should be given different curricula and learning opportunities, thereby leaving some permanently behind and others permanently ahead. Instead, schools are expected to fulfill their obligation of equipping all students with the competence and qualities needed to face the challenges beyond the schoolhouse door. Furthermore, the purposes imply that schools will have to change how they have been operating in order to accomplish this obligation.

11. What are OBE's three premises?

OBE's two purposes described in question 10 are based on three key assumptions or premises, backed by voluminous research and over 30 years of educators' practice. They are:

- All students can learn and succeed, but not on the same day in the same way.

- Successful learning promotes even more successful learning.

- Schools control the conditions that directly affect successful school learning.

The first premise explicitly takes differences in students' learning rates and learning styles into account — not as barriers to successful learning, but as factors that must be designed into any sound instructional process.

It is a very optimistic view of the learning potential of all students. The second premise stresses that successful learning rests on students having a strong cognitive and psychological foundation of prior learning success. The stronger schools can help make both foundations, the easier it will be for students to continue learning successfully. Finally, those who implement OBE believe they are capable of changing how they operate to allow and encourage all students to be successful learners. Schools can function differently than in the past if educators and others who work with them choose to implement needed changes.

Together, these three premises serve as the rationale on which the actual implementation of OBE — guided by its four principles described below — ultimately rests.

12. What are OBE's four principles?

To put the two purposes and three premises into action, those who implement OBE deliberately and consistently guide what they do around four clear principles of decision making and action. These four principles are the heart of OBE. Working together, they strengthen the conditions enabling students and teachers to be successful. Figure 1.3 states these four principles, known in shorthand form as: Clarity of Focus, Expanded Opportunity, High Expectations, and Design Down.

As these four principles can be applied in many ways to achieve OBE's purposes, it makes little sense to think of schools or districts having to implement "THE ONE MODEL" of OBE. Many implementation options are available. However, successful

---

FIGURE 1.3

OBE's "POWER" PRINCIPLES

1. CLARITY OF FOCUS
on Culminating Exit
Outcomes of Significance

2. EXPANDED OPPORTUNITY
and Support for
Learning Success

3. HIGH EXPECTATIONS
for All To Succeed

4. DESIGN DOWN
from Your Ultimate,
Culminating Outcomes

OBE practitioners apply the principles in four ways: consistently, systematically, creatively, and simultaneously.

These criteria for applying the principles contribute directly to a system's effectiveness. In particular, the creative application contributes to a system's capacity to innovate and expand the range of OBE implementation possibilities, which enhances the OBE concept and stimulates continued refinement and evolution.

13. How exactly does OBE's clarity of focus principle work?

This first principle is the most important and fundamental of the four. Nothing can proceed in an authentically outcome-based way without it. Figure 1.4 captures the meaning and spirit of this principle in a series of two-word phrases that indicate how clarity of focus guides instructional planning and delivery.

First, clarity of focus helps educators establish a clear picture of the learning they want students to exhibit in a performance demonstration. Second, student success on this demonstration becomes the top priority for instructional planning and student assessment. Third, the clear picture of the desired outcome is the starting point for curriculum, instruction, and assessment planning and implementation, all of which must perfectly match (or align with) the targeted outcome. And fourth, the instructional process in the classroom begins with the teacher sharing, explaining, and modeling the outcome on day one and continually thereafter, so that the "no surprises" philosophy of OBE can be fully realized. This enables students and their teacher to work together as partners toward achieving a visible and clear goal.

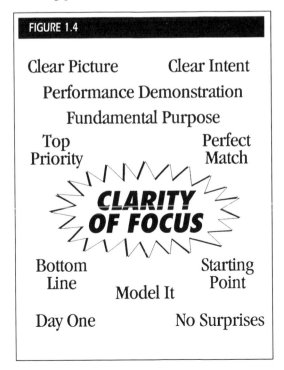

FIGURE 1.4

Clear Picture   Clear Intent
Performance Demonstration
Fundamental Purpose
Top   Perfect
Priority   Match

CLARITY
OF FOCUS

Bottom   Starting
Line   Point
Model It
Day One   No Surprises

14. Does clarity of focus mean all teachers must have the same focus and use the same methods?

No, but this "no" needs some explaining. Outcome-based systems exist to ensure that all students will emerge as successful learners on outcomes deemed essential to their future. This does not mean, however, that one uniform program of study will be pursued at the same time in the same way. The same set of outcomes can be pursued via a variety of approaches and methods, and OBE teachers are continuously encouraged to explore better ways of designing and delivering instruction, especially in light of differences in student learning rates and styles.

Moreover, OBE systems can easily allow students to pursue areas of learning that extend or complement the core framework of exit outcomes — and to pursue those areas in great depth if they desire. So, on the one hand, the overall focus on exit outcomes gives OBE systems a very clear purpose and direction, but the expanded opportunity principle (described below) encourages flexibility in how students can reach and extend beyond those particular outcomes.

15. How exactly does OBE's expanded opportunity principle work?

At its most basic level, expanded opportunity requires staff to give students more than one chance to learn important things and to demonstrate that learning. Initially, those who implemented OBE applied this approach to small segments of learning that students could accomplish in relatively short amounts of time.

But the definition of outcomes and their demonstration has expanded dramatically over the past decade, which has forced a rethinking of the entire concept of opportunity and how it is structured and implemented in schools. At least five dimensions of opportunity now seem directly relevant to this question, and time is only one of them. The five dimensions are listed in Figure 1.5.

As the figure clearly suggests, Time, Methods and Modalities, Operational Principles, Performance Standards, and Curriculum Access and Structuring are all significant aspects of providing and expanding students' opportunities for learning and success. Each of these dimensions is described below.

Dimensions of Opportunity

Time. As it relates to time, the concept of opportunity in schools takes three distinct forms:

- *Teaching Time:* The amount of access and direct support for learning the system offers students.

- *Learning Time:* The amount of time the system gives students before telling them it's too late to learn something.

- *Eligibility:* The window of time the system allows for students to learn particular curriculum components.

FIGURE 1.5

Five Key Dimensions of Opportunity

1. Time

2. Methods and Modalities

3. Operational Principles

4. Performance Standards

5. Curriculum Access and Structuring

From an OBE perspective, all three dimensions can be expanded greatly beyond the traditional system's constraints to ensure that students learn successfully. Furthermore, these forms can be enhanced in three ways, namely, by expanding:

- The duration of learning opportunities

- The frequency of those opportunities

- The precise timing of when those opportunities can occur.

The key to what some call "Outcome-Based Restructuring" is to redefine and reorganize the patterns of teaching time, learning time, and eligibility in schools by expanding their duration, frequency, and/or timing.

That means treating the clock, schedule, and calendar as ways to organize and coordinate teaching and learning opportunities, rather than as rigid definers of those experiences.

Methods and modalities. The concept of opportunity goes far beyond time and timing. One of those dimensions involves the methods and modalities of instruction. This approach is nothing new to educators: They've been talking for two decades about different ways to decipher and work effectively with different "learning styles" and "teaching modalities."

In the 1990s, Harvard professor Howard Gardner's work on what he calls "The Seven Intelligences" has received a great deal of attention — and given teachers yet another tool for tapping into a broader range of student interests and capabilities. Gardner's framework distinguishes seven dimensions of mental functioning and talent inherent in all people: linguistic, logical-mathematical, spatial, musical, bodily-kinesthetic, inter-personal, and intrapersonal. For teachers, using several methods and instructional modalities could expand opportunities for successful learning more than simply manipulating the various dimensions of time.

Operational principles. A third critical dimension of opportunity relates to OBE's other three principles: clarity of focus, high expectations, and design down. Opportunity for learning success will expand enormously if teachers apply these principles consistently, systematically, creatively, and simultaneously in their classrooms. Clarity of focus enhances opportunity by establishing a clear target for learning performance. High expectations opens students' motivational channels and their access to success. Design down provides a clear path for students to pursue and achieve desired learning.

Performance standards. A fourth dimension is imbedded in how performance standards are defined and implemented. Chapter 2 will explain how comparative/competitive standards systems inherently limit some students' chances for success, no matter how high their actual performance levels might be. But criterion-based systems — such as the Scout's merit badge system — clearly define and apply the same standard for all students and impose no limits on how many students can reach a given performance level. This kind of standards system is key to enabling all students to succeed eventually.

Curriculum access and structuring. A fifth dimension of opportunity relates to student access to significant curriculum and resources and to how those curricular experiences are structured. At a very basic level, opportunity is tied to students having access to essential learning experiences and resources. If schools do not make essential courses and programs available to students, or if access is limited to fixed, single-chance events and time blocks, then students' chances for learning and future success are inherently constrained.

On the other hand, if opportunities for critical learning experiences occur repeatedly at ever higher levels of complexity throughout a student's career, the likelihood of continuous improvement and deep internalization of the learning increases. Students are less likely to internalize single, stand-alone curriculum events into their repertoire of useable knowledge and competence.

16. Does expanded opportunity mean students can take as long as they want to learn something or to complete their work?

No, not without consequences. The expanded opportunity principle should not and does not operate in isolation from the other principles. Clarity of focus and high expectations clearly define what is expected of students. In outcome terms, students must do more than perform tasks on schedule to be "finished" or "done." They must perform all criteria of a defined performance to a defined standard. If the standard is not met, the student is still responsible for meeting it. The conditions that must be met to "earn" an expanded opportunity to perform at a higher level must be established at the outset of a learning experience.

The ground rules governing how this principle will be applied should reflect the tension and inconsistencies among student learning rates, effort, delivery schedules, timeliness, and appearances of procrastination. Ultimately, all of these factors revolve around grading: What constitutes a grade? And what must the student do to get one? While this is a crucial political and emotional topic for all students, educators, and parents, it cannot be resolved definitively here. This is partly because typical grading practices, as explained in Chapter 2, may have nothing to do with meeting a set of culminating performance criteria. Nonetheless, seven useful starting points for addressing this issue are outlined on the next page.

1) Whenever possible, OBE educators make a clear distinction between whether students are doing routine assignments or developing ultimate performance capabilities.

2) Educators also differentiate between practice and "ultimate performances." While practice is a necessary route to performance, it is not the performance itself.

3) OBE often differentiates between "pencil" and "ink" grades. A pencil grade is a mark of record that can be changed when improved learning and performance warrants it. Ink grades imply permanent, unchangeable performance status.

4) Many OBE districts expect students to earn the right to receive expanded opportunities by having them consistently do the work and practice that make improvement possible. They do not have automatic second and third chances to do something of consequence.

5) Other districts hold students to a final performance standard in a course or program and consider their work to be incomplete until they meet that standard. Course and/or graduation credit is tied directly to meeting the standard.

6) Many districts do everything possible to make student work so interesting and compelling that lack of engagement and procrastination are eliminated.

7) Student procrastination does not reduce the expectation for what is to be done well. It simply delays the time of completion — a circumstance that educators typically call "failure" and that students usually want to avoid.

17. How exactly does OBE's high expectations principle work?

Simply stated, high expectations means increasing the level of challenge to which students are exposed and raising the standard of acceptable performance they must reach to be called "finished" or "successful." As noted in Figure 1.6, OBE systems have applied this principle to three distinct aspects of school practice: standards, success quotas, and curriculum access.

First, most OBE systems have raised the standard of what they will accept as completed or passing work. This is done, of course, with the clarity of focus, expanded opportunity, and design down principles operating. As a result, students are held to a higher minimum standard than ever before.

Second, most OBE systems have changed their thinking about how many students can or should be successful. They have abandoned bell-curve or quota grading systems in favor of criterion-based systems, and this change of perspectives and practice reinforces the previous strategy.

Third, realizing most

FIGURE 1.6

Three Key Dimensions of High Expectations

1. Raising Standards of Acceptable Performance

2. Eliminating Success Quotas

3. Increasing Access to High-Level Curriculum

students will rise only to the level of challenge they are afforded, many OBE systems have eliminated low-level courses, programs, or learning groups from their curriculum. Experience shows (and the examples in Chapter 5 verify) that applying these dimensions of high expectations: standards, success quotas, and curriculum access, alters a school's learning climate and ethos — and results in higher student achievement in more challenging levels of learning.

18. How do high expectations relate to having and enforcing high standards?

While the two concepts are closely related, high expectations and high standards are different. High expectations implies a desire to have students perform at higher levels, and working with them to increase the likelihood that it happens. On the other hand, a school might simply raise standards without increasing expectations for students or wanting to have more students be successful. But this version of high standards only increases the probability that more students will be unable to meet them. In other words, it raises the barrier to success and decreases the number of students able to surpass it.

19. How exactly does OBE's design down principle work?

Design down means staff begin their curriculum and instructional planning where they want students to ultimately end up and build back from
there. This challenging but powerful process becomes clear when we
think of outcomes as falling into three broad categories: culminating,
enabling, and discrete.

Culminating outcomes define what the system wants all students to be
able to do when their official learning experiences are complete. In fully
developed OBE systems, the term "culminating" is synonymous with exit
outcomes. But in less fully developed systems, culminating might apply to
what are called program outcomes and course outcomes.

Enabling outcomes are the key building blocks on which those culminating outcomes depend. They are truly essential to students' ultimate performance success. Discrete outcomes, however, are curriculum
details that are "nice to know" but not essential to a student's culminating outcomes.

The design down process is governed by the "Golden Rules" shown in
Figure 1.7 and uses the terms just defined. At its core, the process
requires staff to start at the end of a set of significant learning experiences
— its culminating point — and determine which critical components and
building blocks of learning (enabling outcomes) need to be established so
that students can successfully arrive there. The term "mapping back" is
often used to describe this first golden rule. The second rule states that
staff must be willing to replace or eliminate parts of their existing programs that are not true enabling outcomes.

Therefore, the challenges in a design down process are both technical
— determining the enabling outcomes that truly underlie a culminating
outcome — and emotional — having staff be willing to eliminate familiar,
favorite, but unnecessary, curriculum details.

20. Does employing the design down principle mean that important things will be removed from the curriculum?

The second golden rule might make teachers' or publishers' favorite curriculum content unnecessary, optional, or subject to elimination from a
curriculum design. If this content is truly important to students accomplishing significant culminating or enabling outcomes, it must remain in a
curriculum design. But if some curriculum components are peripheral,
they may need to be replaced with more essential things.

FIGURE 1.7

The "Golden Rules" of Outcome-Based Curriculum Design:

Consistently, Systematically, and Creatively:

1. **DESIGN DOWN** from your significant Culminating Outcomes to establish the Enabling Outcomes on which they depend.

2. Replace or delete the Discrete Outcomes that are not significant Enabling components for your Culminating Outcomes.

Clearly, this dilemma must be viewed within the larger context of a district's declared priorities. Design down is a sensible and sound approach to establishing curriculum priorities and structures, provided that implementers have a solid framework of culminating outcomes to guide them.

Theory to practice. A dramatic example of using all the principles with the golden rules was initiated at the Oak Park and River Forest High School in Oak Park, Illinois, in the winter and spring of 1991. At the beginning of the second semester, Richard Deptuch, mathematics division chairperson, took over a class of ninth-grade students who had done poorly in general math during the first semester. His goal was for students to learn the fundamentals of Algebra 1 by the end of the school year. Deptuch's method: the consistent, systematic, creative, and simultaneous use of OBE's four principles, with clarity of focus and design down as the centerpieces.

Deptuch first defined the course's culminating outcome — students would be able to solve quadratic equations successfully. Then he began to redesign the course "back" from there by repeatedly asking himself the question: "What do you have to know and be able to do in order to do that?" With each answer came the need to repeat the question until Deptuch felt satisfied he had established a clear map, designed from the end back, of precisely what students needed to know and do in order to be able to learn the fundamentals of Algebra 1 and ultimately solve quadratic equations. Throughout the semester, clarity of focus, expanded opportunity, and high expectations principles took center stage.

The results of Deptuch's efforts fell into two categories. First, student achievement was exceptional. All of the students in the class passed the full course, and most did extremely well. In June, when Deptuch's students took the school's standardized final exam for the course, the whole class scored in the highest range of nine-month Algebra 1 classes. Struggling general math students had learned Algebra 1 in one semester!

The design down principle gives systems a rigorous way to make what have become increasingly difficult curriculum decisions.

Second, once Deptuch developed his new design down map, he found all available algebra textbooks a hindrance. The books' organization and presentation did not support his design, so he used the book only sparingly throughout the semester. Since his map of the critical enabling outcomes in algebra did not align well with virtually any of the established texts (golden rule 1), he replaced them with his own materials used in his own sequence (golden rule 2) — a brave, necessary, and powerful professional decision.

Overall, then, the design down principle gives systems a rigorous way to make what have become increasingly difficult curriculum decisions. It compels them to examine what is truly essential for their students to accomplish in the limited amount of time a school year or a student's schooling career affords. As the body of knowledge grows rapidly and the demands of the Information Age increase, prudent and insightful curriculum choices become ever more difficult. Basing those choices on a compelling framework of significant outcomes and what will directly help students attain them is preferable to having teachers and students cover more and more material at an increasingly superficial level, with no assurance of a culminating performance ability being the result.

21. Can OBE's four principles be applied in "right" and "wrong" ways in schools and districts?

The four principles can be applied in both structured and flexible ways. They also can be applied to strengthen existing system structures and practices or to alter and expand them significantly. Whether these applications are "right" or "wrong" for a school or district depends primarily on two factors: 1) the types of outcomes a school or district ultimately wants to accomplish and 2) the degree of flexibility given to staff and students to pursue these outcomes.

If districts commit to pursuing outcomes that embody many curriculum skills and details, they will probably interpret and implement the principles from a more micro-perspective. Micro-outcomes lead to micro-curriculum planning, micro-instructional and assessment designs, and micro-thinking about time and opportunity. While this approach can be precise, experience shows it typically leaves a system's time-based constraints in place with the following consequences:

- Teachers and students are bogged down in excessive detail.
- Staff and program flexibility are hindered.
- Learning experiences are segmented.
- Students are less likely to connect school learning with their nonschool lives.
- The kinds of competence students develop is limited.

Conversely, if a district's culminating outcomes have a macro-perspective, requiring years for students to develop and refine, it only makes sense for staff to interpret and apply them on a larger scale. By implication, this macro-approach invites more flexible OBE structuring and implementing, but it has a clear downside. Districts and schools must precisely define their culminating outcomes and carefully develop and assess the enabling outcomes underlying them. Otherwise, staff and students can easily get lost in a sea of generalities and ambiguity. The key is to balance the desire for ultimate macro-results with implementation strategies that ensure critical enabling outcomes are clearly defined, taught, and assessed along the way. This step is one of the most important yet difficult steps facing OBE practitioners.

22. What particular aspects of an education system are based on outcomes and shaped by the four principles?

Let's assume that any educational organization is made up of two broad parts. One is its operational system — the curricular and instructional elements that relate directly to the teaching and learning process. The other is its support system — the administrative, logistical, and resource components that enable the teaching and learning process to exist and function. From this systems perspective, an outcome-based system is one in which exit outcomes and the four principles influence and "drive" all of the key structural and functional components of the operational and support subsystems.

More specifically, assume the operational system is composed of four key parts or structures:

- A standards and accountability structure that determines how achievement and performance standards are defined and how graduation credit is awarded. (This structure includes assessment, grading, report cards, transcripts, credits, and diplomas.)

- A curriculum content and articulation structure that determines how the system's formal learning experiences for students are defined, organized, and linked. (This structure includes programs, courses of study, subject areas, and courses.)

- An instructional process and technology structure that determines what tools and techniques the system uses to engage students in learning the curriculum. (This includes the organization of instruction and the technologies for carrying it out.)

- An eligibility, promotion, and assignment structure that determines which students will work with which teachers and students, on what, when, and under which physical arrangements. (This structure contains everything related to student grouping, scheduling, placement, promotion, and advancement through the curriculum.)

FIGURE 1.8

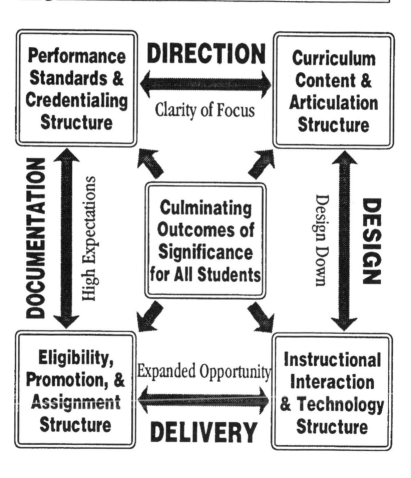

An Outcome-Based Systems Framework

Furthermore, the operational system and its staff are charged with carrying out four broad functions: direction setting, program design, delivery of instruction, and documentation of results. When combined into the systems framework shown in Figure 1.8, these two sets of operational system components provide a more complete answer to question 22.

Note that the four operational structures just defined are represented in the boxes located in the four corners of the diagram. The four operational functions are represented by double-headed arrows connecting the structures. In the center is the box representing the system's ultimate driving force: Culminating Outcomes of Significance for All Students. The arrows of influence emanating from the center box clearly depict the system is outcome-based and outcome-driven.

The four principles contribute to the functioning of the system by directly shaping how each of the four operational functions is carried out. Clarity of focus directly influences direction setting; expanded opportunity directly shapes delivery of instruction; high expectations drives documentation of results; and design down directs the program design function.

Therefore, in a fully developed outcome-based system, all four operational structures and all four operational functions are based on exit outcomes and the four principles, rather than on the clock, calendar, and bell curve. Moreover, in districts that have carried out an outcome-based approach to strategic planning, the support system and its resulting resource priorities and allocations are directly structured around exit outcomes and the four principles as well.

Summary

What are the most important things to remember about what outcome-based education really means?

Later chapters will develop a more detailed picture of how outcome-based systems work. However, here are seven OBE basics to keep in mind:

1) Outcome-based systems are built around outcomes and flexibly use time and other critical resources to accomplish those outcomes for all students.

2) Outcomes are clear demonstrations of learning – not values, attitudes, internal mental processes, or psychological states of mind.

3) Outcomes can take many forms, ranging from specific content skills to complex performances important in life.

4) The kind of outcome-based approach a system implements will be strongly influenced by the kind of outcomes it has defined and is pursuing.

5) Outcome-based models result from the consistent, systematic, creative, and simultaneous application of four key principles to all aspects of a system's decision making and operations.

6) All authentic outcome-based systems make WHAT and WHETHER students learn successfully more important than WHEN and HOW they learn it. This is another way of saying that accomplishing results is more important than providing programs.

7) OBE is NOT a new, experimental idea. Examples of outcome-based models abound in all arenas of society.

Chapter 2
Why Is There So Much Interest in Outcome-Based Reforms?

Although examples of what we now call Outcome-Based Education have been around for centuries and abound in today's world, widespread interest in and advocacy of OBE in schools is a phenomenon of the '90s, and promises to gain even more momentum in the future. Thanks to widespread changes in state education reform policies during the past several years and to the extensive media attention they have received, the term "OBE" has become familiar to tens of millions of Americans.

1. Why is there so much interest in Outcome-Based Education among advocates of major school reforms?

Many who advocate the fundamental reform of our education system find the purposes, premises, principles, paradigm thinking, and results of OBE systems exciting for several reasons:

- The major changes taking place in our economy and society have placed us squarely in the middle of the Information Age.

This complex, technologically dominated, multicultural, constantly changing world demands far higher learning results from schools than they have ever produced. OBE has the inherent potential to meet those demands.

- On the other hand, our Industrial Age educational system embodies and perpetuates patterns of practice that prevent many students from learning successfully. Its emphasis on the means, WHEN, and HOW of educational programs has forced schools to compromise on the ends, WHAT, and WHETHER of student learning. OBE offers the promise of reversing those organizational priorities and patterns.

- OBE shares many philosophies and approaches being used to redefine organizational purpose, processes, and effectiveness in the corporate world. The principles of total quality management, reengineering the organization, systemic change, corporate excellence, and a host of other organizational improvement approaches are all compatible with the philosophies of "all can learn and succeed," "creating the conditions for all to succeed," and "continuous improvement" inherent in OBE.

- Strong examples of outcome-based practice abound in our most important social and economic institutions. Those who are familiar with and have benefitted from OBE's power and common sense in their personal and professional lives want OBE used in schools as well.

- When authentically implemented in a consistent and systematic fashion, OBE lives up to its inherent potential, fostering major improvements in student learning and staff effectiveness in schools and districts of all kinds across the United States. Those who advocate OBE argue that there's no reason why all schools can't emulate what these pioneering OBE districts have accomplished.

- OBE goes beyond the vague symbols, labels, and scores used as indicators of student learning and achievement by the traditional system. Instead, it focuses on and documents the substance of what students have actually learned and can do, and it gives educators, parents, colleges, and future employers a much more accurate picture of students' capabilities.

2. What are some of the key changes taking place in contemporary society and the economy that are directly shaping school reforms?

Three broad, interrelated sets of pressures are affecting the direction and intensity of school reform initiatives in the '90s. They involve, 1) the nature of the Information Age economy and workplace, 2) the changing demographic character of society, and 3) the rate and intensity of change affecting all social and political institutions.

Certainly one of the most compelling descriptions of the changing face of the global economy and workplace is Alvin Toffler's 1991 book, *Power Shifts*. Toffler describes in great detail the impact that continuously emerging technologies are having on what used to be a fairly stable and predictable economic world. That world of "the steady job" and "lifetime career" seems to be over. In its place has emerged the complex, high-technology, competitive, unpredictable, and globally interdependent marketplace that is demanding constant change, adaptation, learning, innovation, and quality from its members. Yesterday's right answers are today's obsolete solutions.

Futurist David Pearce Snyder illustrates the nature of this profound change and its implications for our educational system by pointing out the following:

> While only about 25 percent of the jobs in the post-World War II economy required the reasonably sophisticated handling of information and data, that number has risen to 75 percent in the '90s and is headed for 90 percent by the end of the century. What have traditionally been regarded as "unskilled" and "semi-skilled" jobs now require data manipulation and computer skills.

Beyond this press for an information-literate, technologically competent workforce is an even greater challenge to the educational system: Today's and tomorrow's workers need to be people with high levels of communication, collaboration, interpersonal, and leadership skills! Why? Because, according to several authors and major studies, the hallmark of the Information Age workplace is adaptable, effective working teams that can collectively discover and solve significant problems and work successfully with others to get their potential solutions implemented. Increasingly employers are putting out a seemingly paradoxical message: Technical expertise must be enhanced dramatically, but technical expertise by itself is not enough.

This emphasis on interpersonal skills of all kinds is mirrored in the demographic changes taking place in the United States and Canada. What were regarded 20 years ago as predominantly English-speaking, Anglo societies have become increasingly racially and culturally diverse, thanks to major waves of immigrants from all parts of the world. Consequently, it is common to find the neighborhoods and schools of large cities populated with people representing dozens of different ethnic and home-language backgrounds — all striving to find a niche in the economic, social, and political fabric of their communities.

Compounding these intense pressures for technical competence and interpersonal skills is the rate and intensity of change itself — change in virtually all aspects of life and living. Two implications seem clear. First, people who hope to make their way successfully in this Information Age will have to be motivated, adaptable, and capable of continuous, self-directed, lifelong learning. Second, today's schools are being expected to ensure that those skills and orientations are developed in virtually all students — a tall order for an institution designed a century ago to turn a percentage of its students into literate, reliable workers for the Industrial Age.

3. What are the main Industrial Age features of our educational system that are out of sync with today's Information Age trends and needs?

Two major themes stand out. One is about the system, and the other is about its outcomes. The system issues are best illustrated through one of the themes in the 1982 runaway best seller *In Search of Excellence* by Thomas Peters and Robert Waterman. In it they identify a key characteristic of organizational "excellence" — something they call "Simultaneous Loose-Tight Properties." The excellent corporations they identified had a common characteristic: They were simultaneously tightly focused around organizational goals, purposes, and ends — synonyms for the WHAT and WHETHER discussed in Chapter 1— and loosely organized with regard to means, procedures, and people's roles — synonyms for Chapter 1's WHEN and HOW. Peters and Waterman found just the opposite to be true of what they labeled bureaucratic organizations: The means, procedures, and roles were tight, but the goals, purposes, and ends were loose.

We can identify similar patterns in our Industrial Age model of schooling. There the fixed and tight focus is on programs, time, curriculum, teaching, courses, and schooling itself — all aspects of the means/procedures/roles syndrome. What is loosely defined and highly variable are their ends/purposes/goals counterparts: achievement, standards, performance, learning, criteria, and life respectively.

With regard to learning outcomes themselves, there are similar discrepancies. The Industrial Age model emphasizes the learning of specific curriculum content at specific locations from specific people at specific points in time. Achievement is defined and judged according to how well students can do under those specific, constrained conditions for learning. The Information Age demands long-term, sustainable performance and self-initiated and self-directed continuous learning capabilities, not just specific content and skills for specific tasks. It recognizes that much content becomes quickly obsolete and that the information base with which people must work is expanding beyond the capability of any individual to keep up with and master. As noted earlier, this model emphasizes adaptability, interpersonal competence, and the ability to deal with complex, open-ended issues.

4. What key features of Industrial Age schools inherently constrain learning success for many students?

The traditional, Industrial Age model of schooling operates as a self-contained system. That system is composed of a variety of elements and characteristics that both define what the system is and does and reinforce each other's presence in the system. Ten of those components stand out as critical definers and shapers of how the system operates to limit and constrain the learning opportunities and success of many students. Those key components of the "Time-Based, Industrial Age Paradigm" are listed in Figure 2.1.

FIGURE 2.1

Components of the Time-Based, Industrial Age Paradigm

Calendar-Defined
Constrained Opportunity
Custodial Credentialing
Content Segmentation
Curriculum Coverage
Cumulative Achievement
C'lection Categories
Contest Learning
Comparative Evaluation
Cellular Structure

Calendar-Defined

As the figure suggests, the key characteristic of this paradigm of operating is that it is calendar defined. The nine-month calendar and its components determine what virtually all elements of the system are and how long, how often, and when students will be given opportunities to learn what is in the curriculum. If they don't learn successfully within that schedule, they are declared to be poor learners. Attendance, eligibility, grouping patterns, curriculum, instructional delivery, learning opportunities, assessment and reporting, and student advancement and credentialing are all defined and administered in terms of time.

Constrained Opportunity

Constrained opportunity almost automatically follows because the calendar and schedule place strict limits on the duration and timing of each segment of the educational process. They include: the curriculum structure; opportunities for teachers to teach and students to learn; testing, grading, and reporting student learning (in ink so the grades are permanent); and advancement through the curriculum. All must be done on a fixed schedule, much like the assembly line process of Industrial Age factories. Furthermore, students usually have only one single chance to encounter any learning experience and prove they have "learned" it. The message, intended or not, is: Do it right the first time or suffer the permanent consequences.

Custodial Credentialing

Custodial credentialing refers directly to the system's way of awarding credit for courses completed. The term "custodial" means that students must be in attendance for a fixed period of time to receive credit. "Credentialing" means giving a unit of credit toward the completion of graduation requirements. This is often referred to as a "seat-time" system because the amount of time students spend in their seats in a course is tied directly to how much credit they get. A full Carnegie unit requires 120 hours of sitting; a half credit requires 60. Note that the credit neither documents what students can do nor varies with their performance. Students must simply get a "passing grade" or better to get a Carnegie unit.

Content Segmentation

Content segmentation is a key characteristic of the curriculum and how it is made available to students. The curriculum structure that has dominated 20th century schooling in the United States was recommended by the Committee of Ten in 1893. It is organized around the separate and clearly distinguished academic disciplines of the university — which are treated as if they were distinct and unrelated — and it is further segmented into nine-month chunks called courses and grade levels. Each chunk or segment takes on a life of its own since each has equal status as far as the custodial credentialing system is concerned. Once a nine-month segment is completed and the student has received credit for it, it becomes part of a permanent record, regardless of what is remembered or forgotten.

Curriculum Coverage

Curriculum coverage is the dominant responsibility teachers carry in the system. Their role is to be sure that the content for each curriculum segment is covered or presented to each class within the calendar-defined constraints of the system. This compels teachers to get through the curriculum in the time allowed (WHEN and HOW), regardless of how individual students might do with the material (WHAT and WHETHER). This pressure to cover an expanding body of content within the same time structure that existed a century ago leaves teachers in a no-win bind. Superficial coverage ensures superficial learning, while in-depth treatment leads to missing content. Students lose out either way.

Cumulative Achievement

Cumulative achievement represents the essence of this configuration of components since it defines what the system means by learning and achievement and how it treats them in practice. Two things distinguish this approach to learning and achievement. First, everything students do, regardless of its substance or nature, ultimately is translated into numbers and percentages, which are kept in a student's permanent record. These numeric "symbols" are then endlessly accumulated and averaged together, as if they represented equivalent things — which they clearly do not. Second, once a number is entered into the record it remains there permanently and continues to be a part of the ultimate average. This means any students who start behind or who make mistakes can never actually catch up with the faster starters and "perfect" performers because every mistake remains a part of their accumulated record and average and is permanently held against them — no matter how much or how well they ultimately learn, perform, or improve.

C'lection Categories

The term "C'lection Categories" is a play on words used to maintain the "C" alliteration of the other nine components. C'lection simply means selection — which we regard as the core purpose of this Industrial Age system. The process of sorting and selecting students on the basis of their perceived ability and early achievement translates over time into totally different streams of learning, achievement, and opportunity. It manifests itself first in the "three reading groups" in first grade and continues, however subtly, throughout the elementary years until virtually the same reading group students end up in the college prep, general, and vocational program tracks in high school. This set of practices rests on the premise that not all students can learn the most challenging things in the curriculum, therefore they need lower level challenges and experiences to go with their lower abilities and learning rates. This guarantees that they will fall farther and farther behind and emerge from school destined for very different futures than the "advanced" students.

Contest Learning

One of the surest ways of creating c'lection categories is to set up a system of contest learning in the classroom and school. Unfortunately, contests exist between teachers and students, and between students and students. Why? Because well-meaning educators and policymakers decided a century ago that teachers should only have a limited supply of good grades to dispense because standards of excellence are inherently relative and comparative. This, by definition, forces students who want those symbols of good learning to compete with each other to receive them. The overall distribution of winners and losers is related to a faculty or district's devotion to what is called "the bell curve." Students who are motivated to receive high grades, the symbols of learning success, must compete with others on an individual level. In this competitive environment of learning winners and losers, collaboration is defined as unfair.

Comparative Evaluation

To ensure some form of contest that allows for student selection, the Industrial Age paradigm uses a system of comparative evaluation standards. At its core are principles of interpersonal comparison and ranking. Evaluation focuses on "better than/worse than," "higher than/lower than," and "win/lose" comparisons among students on many different kinds of factors, all of which show up as differences in student performance records, no matter how slight. When these small differences are then turned into the ultimate comparison, class rank, even greater appearances of differences can result — appearances that greatly exaggerate actual differences in learning and performance but make c'lection categories much easier to create and justify. This true, worst-case example occurred on a U.S. university campus in 1992: Students who finished

> **Students who finished a particular course with a 97 average got a D, those who finished with a 98 average got a C, those who finished with a 99 average got a B, and those who got perfect 100 averages got an A.**

a particular course with a 97 average got a D, those who finished with a 98 average got a C, those who finished with a 99 average got a B, and those who got perfect 100 averages got an A.

Cellular Structure

This tenth component of the time-based paradigm relates mainly to its cellular organizational structure — how the programmatic work of teachers and students plays out in physical space. Most teachers work alone all day long and must comply with an externally imposed schedule. Only some receive assistance from aides. Consequently, their work is physically self-contained and programmatically self-constrained. While this physical isolation affords teachers the appearance of a high degree of autonomy and protection from outside interference, it compels individual teachers to be all things to all students, quickly exposes their limitations to students, and confines student learning to what a particular teacher knows and can do. As they work together and reinforce each other systemically, these 10 components make it impossible for many students to become, and be recognized as, successful learners.

5. What are the outcome-based alternatives to these constraining Industrial Age paradigm components?

There are explicit alternatives to each of the 10 key components of the Time-Based, Industrial Age paradigm just described. They are listed in Figure 2.2. When viewed as a whole, these 10 alternatives constitute what we regard as the Outcome-Based, Information Age Paradigm. As might be

---

FIGURE 2.2

Components of the Outcome-Based, Information Age Paradigm

Outcome-Defined

Expanded Opportunity

Performance Credentialing

Concept Integration

Instructional Coaching

Culminating Achievement

Inclusionary Success

Cooperative Learning

Criterion Validation

Collaborative Structure

---

expected, the constellation of these 10 components dramatically expands both teachers' and students' opportunities for achieving genuine success. We will consider them in the order in which they appear.

Outcome-Defined (rather than Calendar-Defined)

As explained in Chapter 1, the outcome-based paradigm is defined, focused, and organized around exit outcomes. These ultimate culminating demonstrations of learning simultaneously serve as the focal point, mission, fundamental purpose, top priority, bottom line, and starting point for everything else that occurs within the system. These things include: designing and developing the curriculum; delivering instruction; assessing, reporting, and credentialing student achievement; determining the criteria for student advancement and eventual graduation; strategic and programmatic decision making; recruiting and using personnel; and structuring and using time and resources.

Expanded Opportunity (rather than Constrained Opportunity)

All systems of instruction and credentialing have within them conditions that define and affect the opportunities of students to be taught, learn successfully, and demonstrate their learning as a matter of record. Expanding opportunities for students to succeed occurs naturally when educators do not define and limit chances for learning and performing to the fixed, prescheduled blocks of time that are the basic structure of our current system's Industrial Age delivery: namely, specific hours, days, weeks, reporting periods, semesters, and school years. The term "expanded" means alterable, variable, flexible, and responsive — not simply longer or more often. As noted in Chapter 1, it pertains to a whole constellation of time factors as well as to the methods, tools, resources, and principles used in instructing and assessing students. Assuring the learning success of all students requires that all of these different aspects of opportunity be expanded and applied well beyond the constraints of the current system.

Performance Credentialing (rather than Custodial Credentialing)

The term "credentialing" refers to many different components that define or reflect the student's standing in the system. They include the design and implementation of assessments, evaluation, record-keeping and transcripts, report cards, the awarding of credit or diplomas, and the advancement or graduation of students. By tying the term "performance" to it, we are indicating that all of these components will be defined by and will directly reflect the clear criteria embodied in a system's culminating outcomes. Therefore, to earn a performance credential, students must clearly demonstrate all of the criteria that constitute that outcome — just as they do in earning merit badges in the Scouts. Performance credentials are defined by these criteria, not by calendar dates or time blocks.

Concept Integration (rather than Content Segmentation)

Curriculum design and structuring proceed directly from a system's framework of culminating outcomes. In more fully developed outcome-based models, these exit outcomes are likely to take the form of complex performance abilities that require students to integrate, synthesize, and apply a range of diverse content, concepts, and competence to performance tasks. Without question, this will require them to have learning experiences that continually bring this diversity of content, concepts, and competence together and give students both direct experience and support in seeing how they can be integrated and applied. For this to happen, districts need to develop curriculum designs that continuously link content and concepts together, both across subject areas and grade levels, and that ask students to make and demonstrate those linkages on a continuing basis.

Instructional Coaching (rather than Curriculum Coverage)

Clearly, instructional staff are the key agents for accomplishing OBE's "success for all" purposes. This requires teachers to adopt an orientation to their work that Theodore Sizer (1983) calls an Instructional Coach. Coaches seek to gain the highest quality of performance they can get from all of their musicians, actors, debaters, or athletes. This type of instructional role requires teachers to model actively successful techniques and behavior, continuously diagnose and assess ongoing student practice and performance, offer frequent and focused feedback, and intervene constructively in the learning process in a timely manner. In simple terms, instructional coaching is "effective teaching" at its best. Why make the effort to coach rather than cover? So that the best and most consistent performance of both the individual and the group can occur.

Culminating Achievement (rather than Cumulative Achievement)

Since outcomes are culminating demonstrations of learning, they occur at or after the end of a learning process and embody its ultimate results. By focusing on true outcomes, rather than on just their enabling objectives, educators are compelled to shift their focus on what students learn from "during" to "after" and from discrete micro-performances to ultimate applications of prior learning experiences. Culminating achievement is the ultimate "So what?" of all the things students do on a daily basis to develop and improve their learning. It is the highest level performance and the final result of all of their prior learning and practice, not the average of all of that prior learning. And it is what they are able to do successfully as they exit the system and enter the world beyond high school. Having students leave the system with significant, demonstrable capabilities is the essence of the outcome-based paradigm, and it embodies the system's purpose, mission, priorities, starting point, and ultimate measure of effectiveness.

Inclusionary Success (rather than C'lection Categories)

Outcome-based systems define and structure their operations around outcomes of significance because they want all of their students to succeed at them. By consistently, systematically, creatively, and simultaneously applying the four principles to everything they do, outcome-based systems continuously demonstrate their commitment to creating and sustaining the conditions that make inclusionary success possible. This component embodies the spirit and intent of OBE's key purposes and serves as the key shaper of the other nine components. Consequently, OBE systems impose no quotas on which or how many students can be successful, nor do they limit what students will be allowed to learn and how high they can aspire. In addition, they oppose the Industrial Age system's implementation of permanent grouping or tracking structures and bell-curve thinking and practices.

Cooperative Learning (rather than Contest Learning)

When a system is committed to having all of its students succeed on clearly defined performance standards, it focuses on finding and fostering effective ways for that to happen. Consequently, those who implement OBE work to transform the notion of competition into a reality called "continuous high-level challenge" for all students. In a criterion-based system of standards and expectations, no one has to lose just because others succeed sooner. The reasons?   Because OBE is essentially a win/win model, and success is not a scarce, fixed commodity. Coaches know that group performance is tied directly to the ability of the weakest member of the group. Smart coaches get everyone into the act of helping everyone else get better so that the performance of everyone is enhanced in the process. When teachers do it, it's called "peer coaching." When applied to students, it's called cooperative learning. For centuries it's also been known as teamwork and collaboration.

Criterion Validation (rather than Comparative Evaluation)

First, a criterion is an essential component of a demonstration or performance. It defines what must be present in the performance; otherwise, the performance is judged to be incomplete. A criterion is stated in substantive language that clearly embodies and defines what the essential performance component is. The components that constitute a merit badge in the Scouts are good examples of criteria. Second, the term "validation" means "confirmation" or "verification." When combined, these terms define an approach to assessment, evaluation, and credentialing that requires assessors to gather the most accurate and pertinent information possible on a student's performances and to determine whether that information or evidence matches, meets, or exceeds the criteria that define the essential components of the performance. The essence of this approach is to deal directly with the substance of what is being assessed on its own terms, rather than attaching scores, labels, or symbols to it. The performance of other students on the same criteria should have no bearing on the assessment made. This makes the terms "authentic assessment" and criterion validation virtually identical. They both involve validly assessing exactly what the outcome demonstration requires.

Collaborative Structure (rather than Cellular Structure)

The exit outcomes that drive advanced OBE systems usually involve complex, high-level performances that go beyond the content and skills addressed in individual courses or program areas. These complex abilities, like communicating and complex problem solving, take years to develop, refine, and apply. They are not something that students acquire or develop in days, weeks, or months while enrolled in particular courses or grade levels. Their development depends on the continuing efforts of all teachers in all areas of the curriculum. Hence, all teachers have a stake in helping students achieve the system's exit outcomes. For that to happen, they must work together to invent and implement the learning experiences and strategies that will allow this kind of complex performance ability to emerge. Staff are compelled to build lines of communication and collaboration across traditionally impenetrable content and grade-level boundaries because good ideas, effective strategies, and focused endeavors can, and must, come from everywhere and everyone.

As they work together and reinforce each other systemically, these ten components establish the conditions that enable all students to become, and be recognized as, successful learners.

6. How do these OBE components relate to the total quality and reengineering movements in American business?

During the past two decades, the corporate world has undergone a profound transformation in its approach to organization and management that parallels the educational paradigm shift just described. This transformation embodies the shift from an Industrial Age to an Information Age way of defining and operating business enterprises in the volatile and challenging environment described in Toffler's *Power Shifts*. The hallmark of this shift is the notion of:

> Establishing within the organization the conditions that motivate and empower individuals to use the potential that is within them.

If Peters and Waterman's *In Search of Excellence* can be used as a benchmark, this transformation is simply a decade ahead of what is now happening in education. Among the most widely recognized work and figures in this movement to empower people and transform the organizations in which they work are:

> Joel Barker's *The Business of Paradigms* (1990);
>
> Stephen Covey's *The Seven Habits of Highly Effective People* (1989); and *Principle-Centered Leadership* (1990);
>
> Michael Hammer and James Campy's *Reengineering the Corporation* (1993);
>
> Thomas Kuhn's *The Structure of Scientific Revolutions* (1970); and
>
> Peter Senge's *The Fifth Discipline* (1990).

Of course, the legendary work of the late W. Edwards Deming addressed the principle of applying profound knowledge to the continuous improvement of organizational and product quality.

The focus on the potential of all individuals to perform successfully, the emphasis on success for all, the theme of establishing within organizations the conditions that allow and encourage individuals to do their best, the breaking of counterproductive mindsets and organizational patterns, the defining of organizational purpose as "achieving quality everywhere," the notion of principle-driven action, and the concept of organizational flexibility as a means for achieving clearly defined, high-quality ends are among the most obvious examples of the direct connection between empowering outcome-based educational systems and what we might think of as empowering outcome-based corporations.

7. What features of outcome-based models in daily life appeal so strongly to education reformers?

The models of outcome-based practice introduced in Figure 1.1 (Chapter 1) have an enormous appeal to education reformers because they illustrate the powerful, commonsense simplicity of OBE. They also reveal a range of possibilities for focusing and organizing instruction that goes beyond the institutionalized constraints of our Industrial Age system described in Figure 2.1. Some of the most inherently appealing features of these everyday examples of outcome-based practice are:

- Learning results and performance expectations are clearly defined ahead of time.

- Learners know what they are expected to learn, and instructors know what to help them learn.

- There are no surprises in what is to be learned and what will be assessed. What you see is what you get.

- If learning is clearly defined and instruction takes the learner's experience, learning style, and learning rate into account, almost anyone can learn anything that is truly essential to his or her success and well-being.

- Clear standards for being "done" and receiving official certification are tied to consistent, quality accomplishments and performance.

- Few can learn complex things the first time they try. Continual practice and coaching are essential to the development of significant competence.

- It makes sense to design curriculum back from where you want your learners to successfully end up.

- Advancement in learning is tied directly to actual levels of successful performance, not to a fixed schedule. Learners can move through a curriculum successfully at a pace they can handle.

- Outcome-based performance credentials are like "truth in advertising." They prove what learners can do.

8. How does OBE provide parents and the public with more accurate and meaningful information about student learning and capabilities than do conventional systems?

Few issues are as emotionally and politically charged as those dealing with student grades and credentials. This is largely because during the past three decades a person's career/life chances have become increasingly linked to the kind of educational background and credentials he or she has. Outcome-based systems offer parents and the public two things: 1) a major enhancement of opportunities for students to learn the things that would qualify them for admission to advanced levels of education and improve their chances of being successful once they are there, and 2) credentials and transcripts that accurately document what they can successfully do when they exit the K-12 system.

Grades as Vague Symbols of Achievement

While reformers embrace both these reasons, the public generally finds them confusing. For several generations, Americans have been immersed in a particular way of assessing, labeling, and credentialing student achievement, which OBE practice regards as vague and misleading. The issues come down to a choice between numbers and symbols versus substance and criteria. From an outcome-based perspective, the heart of the dilemma of how to define and report student achievement comes down to the following paradox:

As substance, grades mean nothing!
As symbols, grades mean everything!

To support the first part of this argument, OBE advocates point to two realities. One is captured in the alliterative message in Figure 2.3, which illustrates grades as an uninterpretable mixture of incredibly dissimilar things, all of which are filtered through the particular perspectives, priorities, and preferences of individual teachers. From an outcome-based perspective, "Accomplishments" is the only one of the seven factors in Figure 2.3 that begins to conform to what an outcome is. From a simple systemic perspective, grades are not valid or reliable measures of achievement because no two teachers' grades mean the same thing!

FIGURE 2.3

Grades Are Accumulated Amalgamations of:

Accomplishments
Activities
Assignments
Attendance
Attitudes
Aptitudes
Averages

The second major reality surrounding grades is illustrated in what are called "The Five Great Illusions of Achievement" shown in Figure 2.4. These illusions center on the belief that scores and numbers actually are students' achievements.

These great illusions also illustrate that the entire expectations system surrounding student learning and performance is disturbingly low. In most districts the passing standard of 70 percent is dramatically below what people like Deming or the Boy Scouts would define as "quality." Furthermore, the chances are very high that most students never learn to do very many things at really high levels of quality because the points system doesn't encourage or require it. So, rather than grades being objective indicators or measures of achievement as the traditional educational system claims, the combination of these two realities reveals them to be:

FIGURE 2.4

The Five Great
ILLUSIONS
of Achievement

1. Everything is worth 100 points!

2. All points are created equal!

3. If students don't perform successfully, take points off!

4. Seventy (or eighty, or ninety) points is good enough!

5. The more points you accumulate, the more achievement you have!

Uninterpretable symbolic or numeric labels reflecting the subjective judgments of individual teachers about dissimilar, unrelated things that occurred during a specific time period.

Criterion-Based Reporting

Those who advocate OBE believe that students, parents, and the public deserve something better. Their approach has strong parallels to the criterion-based nature of the merit and honor badge system in the Scouts because it focuses on, records, and reports the actual substance and levels of what students can do at any given point in time. This approach would allow parents and the public to receive five extremely valuable kinds of information on a regular basis:

- What the system's key culminating and enabling outcomes are for all its students. (This establishes the framework on which all curriculum design, formal assessment, credentialing, and reporting will be done.)

- What the substantive criteria are for each level of performance on those outcomes. (This establishes the actual meaning of performance standards for each outcome.)

- Where a particular student falls on the range of levels for each outcome on a given reporting date. (This is the current report of the student's performance levels.)

- Where that student fell on the range of performance levels on some previous reporting date. (This documents the student's progress and improvement on the outcome over time.)

- Where other similar students fall on the range of performance levels for each outcome. (This provides data on the student's performance relative to that of other students.)

9. What do those implementing OBE find attractive about its cost and effectiveness?

While we will develop this point more extensively in Chapter 5, five major points can be summarized here. These benefits usually result from the determined efforts of both formal and informal leaders on the staff to make a difference where it really counts, sometimes at the expense of changing or abandoning long-revered practices and organizational rituals that prove to be unproductive in the face of better options.

Purpose and direction. First, OBE gives districts a much clearer purpose and sense of direction than ever before. This occurs through a process called "Strategic Design," in which districts and their communities establish a clear mission, a vision of how they will conduct their affairs, a framework of values and principles that guide decision making, a framework of exit outcomes that guide program design and priorities, and a strategic plan for allocating resources and using staff that is consistent with the defined mission, vision, values, and exit outcomes. This process translates directly into the classroom through the clarity of focus and design down principles.

More consistency. Second, because of OBE's purposes, principles, and exit outcomes, there is a much clearer rationale for, and more consistency in, all policy and programmatic decisions that are made. The four principles serve as particularly powerful guides for both decision making and action in the short term and longer run.

Increased motivation and morale. Third, student motivation and achievement, as well as staff effectiveness and morale, typically increase well beyond previous experience and expectations. This results in a significant shift in organizational climate, shared sense of empowerment, improved relationships, and heightened expectations for greater success. At times, previously insurmountable problems find ready solutions because of people's greater willingness to address them openly.

Improved school-community relations. Fourth, relations between the school and its community improve as the result of two key things: 1) authentic involvement in the district's direction-setting process and 2) improved student motivation and achievement — both of which greatly enhance the system's credibility with its public. These closer ties have mutually reinforcing benefits as communication and confidence build in both directions.

Effectiveness worth the cost. Fifth, sound OBE is generally no more expensive to implement day-to-day than less-focused traditional practices. While a greater percentage of a district's budget may be needed for staff and program development under OBE, most districts usually find these funds by saving in other parts of the budget. From a cost/effectiveness point of view, sound OBE implementation is a major benefit to students and to taxpayers.

Summary

What are the most important things to remember about the intense interest being expressed in OBE today? As we proceed to examine outcome-based models and practices in more detail, it is important to keep in mind these five key points about the widespread interest in OBE:

1) OBE embodies the commonsense thinking and practice of effective instructional design and delivery found in highly effective learning systems throughout our society.

2) Outcome-based models respond to a clear need in our society for learning systems that promote rather than constrain the learning opportunities of all students; they all will need to be prepared for the continuous learning and improvement challenges of the Information Age labor market.

3) The transformation of our society from Industrial Age to Information Age realities and needs has fundamentally affected the nature of work and employment opportunities. Competence in information processing and data handling is already essential in most jobs today.

4) OBE has strong parallels with the "quality revolution" taking place throughout the business world.

5) OBE is geared to providing concrete, useful information to parents, employers, and colleges regarding the actual performance abilities of students and the improved effectiveness of the system — all within reasonable and responsible operating budgets.

Chapter 3
What Are Outcomes and How Are They Derived?

N othing is more fundamental to understanding and implementing Outcome-
Based Education than defining outcomes
themselves. This chapter examines some
of the most important issues surrounding
the meaning of outcomes and how they
are derived.

1. What are outcomes?

As noted early in Chapter 1, outcomes "happen." They are the learning
results we desire from students that lead to culminating demonstrations.
These results and their demonstrations occur at or after the end of a significant learning experience; hence the term "culminating." This means
that an outcome is not a collection or average of previous learning experiences, but a manifestation of what learners can do once they have had and
completed all of those experiences. This also means that outcomes are not
simply the things students believe, feel, remember, know, or understand —
these and other similar things are all internal mental processes, rather than
clear demonstrations of learning. Instead, outcomes are what students
actually can do with what they know and understand.

To solidify these critical points, consider the items listed as "Outcome Aliases" in Figure 3.1. This list includes a number of things people readily confuse with outcomes, including values, attitudes, goals, scores, and averages. But none of these items, either singly or in combination, conforms to the definition provided here and in Chapter 1. Nothing is more fundamental in understanding OBE in its authentic forms than these distinctions. However, like most

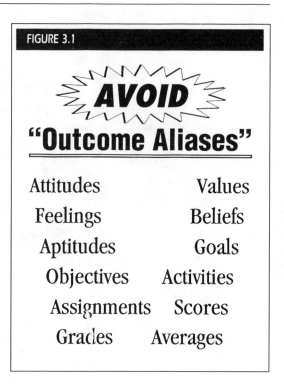

FIGURE 3.1

AVOID
"Outcome Aliases"

Attitudes	Values
Feelings	Beliefs
Aptitudes	Goals
Objectives	Activities
Assignments	Scores
Grades	Averages

things in education, outcomes can vary a great deal along a series of dimensions, all of which affect their overall significance to learners and the schools they attend. Many of these dimensions will be explored and explained as the chapter progresses.

2. What is the difference between an outcome and an "outcome of significance"?

The term "outcome of significance" began to be used by some of the leading implementers of OBE in the mid-1980s. These individuals came to recognize that a great many of the examples of outcomes being pursued in those days were micro-skills and isolated bits of information that were of little consequence to students and their teachers once the immediate learning experience was completed, tested, and recorded in the teacher's book. Often they represented small bits of information and parts of isolated segments of curriculum that students quickly forgot once that curriculum segment was completed. Typical examples include the names of the lead characters in a novel or the names of the tributaries of a river.

The initial outcomes of significance notion was that if outcomes were worth pursuing and accomplishing, they should embody things that:

- Students would remember and be able to do long after a particular curriculum episode ended

- Were truly important to students in their educational and life-career futures.

In other words, outcomes needed to be things that really mattered to students and for students in the long run, and educators were encouraged to design their programs accordingly.

3. Is the notion of "significance" related to the term "culminating"?

Yes, definitely! What implementers of OBE began to realize once this notion of "really mattering in the long run" began to gel was that an enormous amount of daily learning never makes it to the end of any significant time period, let alone beyond it. This starts with not being able to do on Monday what was required on the previous Friday's test, and it simply compounds as time goes on. Listing specific facts about a rarely encountered phenomenon and spelling last week's words are classic examples of quickly forgotten details.

As OBE implementers grappled with this dilemma, a clear distinction gradually emerged. It separated short-term content learning — what students often must do in each segment of the curriculum to get a grade — from the development of internalized performance abilities — what students will carry with them throughout and beyond their formal schooling that cannot be developed inside of any single segment of curriculum. Designing and carrying out research projects is a case in point; it takes years of study and practice to be able to do it well.

Finding meaning. The more OBE teachers and administrators examined this distinction, the more they realized that a great deal of school learning doesn't make it to graduation night, let alone beyond it. As educators approached what seemed to be the increasingly formidable task of defining and implementing outcomes, this distinction challenged them to ask of everything they considered: "So what difference will learning this make in the long run?" After years of hard work and analysis, three realizations that reflect the common sense inherent in OBE emerged. They were:

1) The closer a demonstration of learning falls near the "real" end of a student's learning experiences, the more likely the learning is to carry over into other experiences — especially if it includes components that the student practiced extensively over a lengthy period of time and would use again once he or she was "finished."

2) Graduation is the ultimate "culminating point" in a student's career. If it's really important that students take something out the door with them, this "exit point" is the time to make sure it's there.

3) Students can't take out the door what they haven't been taught and had the opportunity to use and practice extensively while they were "inside."

4. If the term "culminating" ultimately refers to the end of a student's school career, does that mean that everything learned earlier really doesn't matter?

Not at all, but it does compel educators to examine carefully how they design learning experiences for students so they can develop and practice both the content and performance abilities critical to their future success. This raises two key issues.

First, it highlights the importance of OBE's design down principle and the golden rules of curriculum design discussed in Chapter 1 — particularly the distinctions made among culminating, enabling, and discrete outcomes. Based on what we have just discussed and the ideas that will be developed later in this chapter, it is extremely important for those implementing OBE to begin with the most significant culminating outcomes possible — things like complex communications abilities and research and planning abilities — and then design their curricula back from there. This will assure that students have extensive experience throughout their school years with both increasingly complex forms of the culminating outcomes themselves and with the genuine enabling outcomes on which they depend. That design strategy may compel those who implement OBE to eliminate some elements in the current curriculum that prove simply to be isolated content details and discrete objectives in the new framework.

Second, it calls into question the usefulness and relevance of using permanent grading and averaging as a way of documenting student outcomes, both for individual learning experiences and courses, as well as for the program of study as a whole. Why? Because as noted in the latter part of Chapter 2, grades are accumulations of time-specific things that happen well before the "real end" occurs. If anything, grades may reflect something about students' initial performances on discrete objectives and some enabling outcomes. But culminating outcomes occur after all of the grading and averaging is finished. As the principal of a Kansas City high school stated in 1990:

> All the grades in my school will be in pencil until graduation
> night, because no student is going to be given the message that
> it is too late to improve his or her learning on something we
> have taught.

In other words, he was supporting the notion that the real definition of student learning and achievement is how well students can do things after they have had extended opportunity to practice and improve. The first time through is not an adequate indication of what students will ultimately be able to do. Nor will it necessarily "stick" unless reinforced and practiced on a continuing basis.

5. Does this mean that specific content and skills are unimportant to those implementing OBE?

Certainly not. Among other things, OBE's high expectations principle advocates giving all students stimulating, challenging, in-depth encounters with high-level areas of knowledge and skills. And the golden rules of design down require that staff build into their curricula both the knowledge and competence bases that are critical for students to develop and ultimately apply.

But, by the same token, those knowledgeable about OBE are careful to distinguish between content and skills that are important in enriching students' lives and those they know are truly essential for students to develop into high-level performers on a framework of culminating outcomes. Furthermore, they recognize that people forget content details and specific skills very quickly if they are not used regularly and tied to important concepts and experiences that have real meaning. Consequently, in applying the golden rules of design down, OBE practitioners will inevitably weigh curriculum choices heavily against the educational "rock and hard place": the rapid expansion of knowledge in all fields, the changing demands of the high-tech marketplace, and the fixed amount of time the system allows for dealing with any curriculum content, old or new.

6. What specifically goes into a demonstration of learning?

Another way to ask the question is to equate the term "demonstration of learning" with the term "performance." What goes into a successful performance? One way of looking at it is through "The Learning Performance Pyramid" illustrated in Figure 3.2. While the components in the pyramid are quite general, they make this basic point: To perform successfully people have to 1) have something to perform; 2) be able to carry out a performance process; and 3) be willing, motivated, and confident enough to carry out the performance under the conditions defined. In other words, they have to KNOW something; be able to DO something with what they know; and BE LIKE a confident, successful performer as they're doing it.

We find examples of this performance pyramid played out constantly in everyday life, but it is particularly visible in areas that involve an audience or people entrusted to the care of others. These include: radio and television newscasters, announcers, interview hosts, actors, public relations professionals, concert and studio musicians, competitive athletes, courtroom lawyers, surgeons, pilots and bus dri-

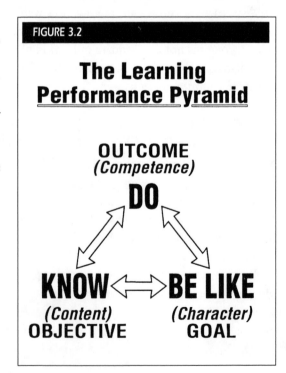

FIGURE 3.2

The Learning Performance Pyramid

OUTCOME
(Competence)

DO

KNOW ⟷ BE LIKE
(Content)   *(Character)*
OBJECTIVE   GOAL

vers, and instructors of all kinds. All of these professionals require a combination of content knowledge, applied competence, and the character attributes of confidence and sound judgment in order to carry out their jobs successfully. The same, of course, can be said for students when placed in performance situations, both within and outside the classroom.

The 3 C's. Extended more fully, the pyramid suggests that a performance requires the integration and application of content, competence, and confidence, and that no one of these three components can be isolated from the others or be a performance in its own right. Knowledge or content by itself is not an outcome, but an enabling instructional objective. Similarly, what is called confidence is, by itself, essentially an educational goal for which students cannot be held specifically accountable. Finally, competence does not exist in isolation from the other two. To become real, it requires both content and the confidence and willingness to perform.

7. Does this mean that outcomes inevitably involve values and other affective factors?

With lots of qualifications and explanation, the answer is "yes." But at least three major issues underlie this affirmative response. First, as we have just seen, performances are influenced by a constellation of things we have called confidence. Among them are things like courage, motivation, willingness, and even "composure under pressure." But other things like attitude, attentiveness, perseverance, inspiration, flexibility, maturity, experience, and self-concept are frequently added to that list by those intimately involved in coaching performers of various kinds. In the eyes of these experts, confidence factors of various kinds cannot be removed from what a quality performance requires.

If this is so, then a series of critical questions concerning these factors arises:

- Do all factors like attitudes, motivation, confidence, and self-concept fall into a category called "psychological/affective states of mind"? Yes, definitely.

- Do all of them have a direct bearing on successful performing? Most certainly. They are vital to any kind of successful learning demonstration.

- Can people function effectively as students or in their lives without them? Highly unlikely.

- Are they "outcomes" in their own right? NO: They simply are a critical ingredient that makes successful outcome demonstrations possible.

Tailored to the community. Second, deriving, developing, or defining outcomes cannot be done without values coming into play because these processes inevitably involve communities and educators having to make choices from among sets of alternatives and possibilities. What gets selected or defined reflects the preferences of those involved in the process — the types of learning they value over other types, often based on their assumed benefits and consequences for the individual and society at large. This matter of selecting preferences applies to any policy or practice involving schools and students, not just to determining outcomes. Again, these matters generate some valid questions:

- Are the values underlying these decisions or actions always explicitly stated? No, often they are simply implied.

- Do they involve deeply felt, personal issues? Often they do, which is why some people get upset when preferences other than their own are chosen.

Third, compounding this set of issues are distinctions between kinds of values: distinctions that often are forgotten or blurred in the heat of controversies. While there are many dimensions to values and many different frameworks for organizing and understanding them, one simple distinction that helps address this larger question separates civic values from personal values.

Civic and personal values

Civic values are those standards of behavior that the members of a total society honor, respect, and even require to enable the society to function in a positive, civil manner. Honesty, respect for the law and the political rights of others, loyalty, fairness, caring, and personal accountability are simple examples. Communities regularly ensure that these civic values are incorporated into their schools, both in the official curriculum and in the celebrations and rituals that go on throughout the school year.

Personal values involve those standards of behavior that honor the religious, moral, and cultural beliefs of particular kinship or social groups. They usually are personally and deeply felt and, at times, clash with those held by the larger society. While this tension between civic and personal values always has existed in public education, OBE can seem to compound it because clearly defined outcomes and the clarity of focus principle simply make explicit and "official" practices that traditionally have been vague and implicit. Disagreement is difficult when things are implied, but much more likely when they are clearly spelled out and public.

Nonetheless, in the face of communities' inherent tension between civic and personal values, plus the confusion and concern surrounding the existence of "attitudinal and affective" factors in demonstrations of learning, OBE is quite explicit about two things:

- Specific values, attitudes, or beliefs are not legitimate outcomes for which students should be held accountable. While communities might feel strongly about their presence in the curriculum and in the ways teachers work with students, they should be treated as goals, not as outcomes.

- The psychological and affective attributes that are an inherent part of any performance also are not outcomes in their own right. Students need them in order to function and perform effectively, but from a design and implementation perspective, they too are best treated as goals, not outcomes.

8. Other than things directly involving values and attitudes, is there a way to distinguish between goals and outcomes?

Yes, and that takes us back to the early part of Chapter 1 as well as the issues raised in Figure 3.3 (see page58), which denote two quite distinct paradigms of learning that currently co-exist within the field of education. The one labeled "psychological' regards learning as the forms and modes of mental processing that go on within the human mind. No learning is possible without these mental processes. The one labeled "sociological" views learning as the ability to translate mental processing into forms and kinds of action that occur in real social settings. This ability to apply mental processing through the use of demonstration processes and verbs (like write, organize, design, or produce) corresponds to the definition of an outcome explained in this book. Outcomes are the forms of learning that we can see students do and that we can directly assess.

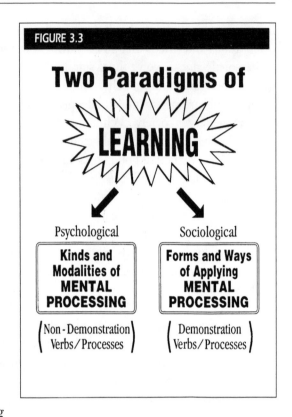

FIGURE 3.3

Two Paradigms of

LEARNING

Psychological

Kinds and Modalities of MENTAL PROCESSING

(Non-Demonstration Verbs/Processes)

Sociological

Forms and Ways of Applying MENTAL PROCESSING

(Demonstration Verbs/Processes)

By contrast, the term "goal" is associated with what we call nondemonstration verbs — verbs that embody or imply internal mental processing of some kind but do not translate directly into observable action. Because the field of education has been dominated by the psychological paradigm during this century, its common mode of discourse in defining and addressing learning is filled with nondemonstration verbs and processes like these:

Know	Understand	Believe	Appreciate
Think	Consider	Reflect	Remember
Assimilate	Acquire	Value	Feel

The issue here is not that those implementing OBE do not want students to know, understand, or appreciate things. It is that it is difficult to tell whether the mental processes coined by these goal terms are indeed operating within the student. As well, it may be unclear what students actually are supposed to do to show that these processes exist.

Without question, one of the most problematic and conflict-producing things in all of OBE is schools and districts using nondemonstration verbs when they define outcomes.

9. What kinds of "real" outcomes are there?

All kinds of terms and labels are used to classify or describe outcomes, and all this variability and inconsistency has led to confusion and misunderstanding among educators and the public. Six of the most common categories of descriptors are listed below:

1) **Content Focus.** Outcomes are classified according to the discipline, subject area, or content they represent. Examples include: mathematics outcomes, social studies outcomes, and reading outcomes.

2) **Time-Referenced.** Outcomes are classified according to the time blocks to which they are linked. Examples include: middle school outcomes, semester outcomes, and grade-level outcomes.

3) **Curriculum Scope.** Outcomes are classified according to the scope of the curriculum segment to which they are linked. Examples include: lesson outcomes, unit outcomes, and program outcomes.

4) **Jurisdictional Domain.** Outcomes are classified according to the organizational jurisdiction that defines them and uses them for accountability or reporting purposes. Examples include: state outcomes, district outcomes, and departmental outcomes.

5) **Competence Complexity.** Outcomes are classified according to the nature, scope, and complexity of the competence that must be used to perform them. Examples include: discrete skills, complex unstructured tasks, and complex role performances.

6) **Operational Function.** Outcomes are classified according to the function they serve within a design framework. Examples include: culminating outcomes, enabling outcomes, and discrete outcomes.

Of these six kinds, the content focus, time-referenced, and curriculum scope categories are used most often in older, more traditional OBE implementation approaches. But as OBE has evolved over the past decade, the competence complexity and operational function frameworks have become much more prevalent. Examples from these latter two categories are used throughout this book to explain the status of many advanced implementation efforts.

10. If there are many different kinds of outcome frameworks, how can a district be sure it is on the right track in defining and pursuing outcomes?

There are two key answers to this question. The first lies in this chapter's earlier discussion of "outcomes of significance." Those involved in a district's outcome derivation process cannot go wrong by focusing on the simple notion of having outcomes be performance abilities that really matter in the long run and making sure that "long run" means well after the students have finished school. A very sound method for developing a compelling rationale for what these abilities should be is called strategic design, which will be described in more detail later in this chapter.

The second answer is related to the simple framework presented in Figure 3.4, called "Three Critical Domains of Outcomes." The framework suggests three things that help answer the question.

First, the largest and most critical domain of outcomes is those relating to students' performance abilities. They are the ones that embody the concept of outcomes presented in this book and that represent the ultimate outcomes of significance just discussed.

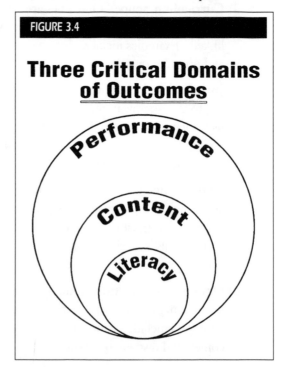

FIGURE 3.4

Three Critical Domains of Outcomes

Performance

Content

Literacy

Second, embedded within those performance outcomes are two other domains of outcomes: content outcomes (which reflect essential core knowledge without which performance is impossible) and literacy outcomes (which represent the language and numeric tools for acquiring knowledge and developing other kinds of competence). As suggested by the diagram, both are critical enablers of performance outcomes, and both are significant in their own right as kinds of learning that really matter in the long run.

Third, districts must be explicit about what they expect and what they are willing to guarantee with respect to all three domains of outcomes, otherwise the public is bound to wonder whether content and literacy explicitly matter in performance-oriented OBE systems. They absolutely do, and their role in the overall framework of district outcomes must be clearly established at the outset.

11. What is the difference between today's performance outcomes and the behavioral objectives of yesteryear?

While there are exceptions to all generalizations, the answer to this question lies within a framework that is commonly used to explain the differences among the types of outcomes that fall into the competence complexity category mentioned earlier. The framework is called "The Demonstration Mountain," and it portrays a picture of six major forms that demonstrations of learning, or competence, take. These forms range from very simple and discrete skills to the very complex and challenging performances people carry out within their life responsibilities and roles. The picture of these six forms appears in Figure 3.5 (see page 62). Each is listed within the body of the Mountain.

When considered as an entire set, these six forms of demonstrations constitute the elements in a hierarchy of performance competence. This directly implies that each form of competence serves as a critical enabler for the forms above it. The words and graphics surrounding the mountain are meant to suggest that the higher one climbs:

- The more complex and significant the demonstrations of learning become.

- The more complex and challenging the settings, circumstances, and contexts in which the demonstration takes place become.

- By implication, the greater the degree of self-direction, motivation, and adaptability required of the learner.

FIGURE 3.5

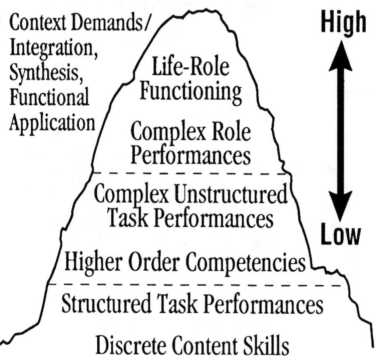

The Demonstration Mountain

Complexity Of:

Context Demands/
Integration,
Synthesis,
Functional
Application

Life-Role
Functioning

Complex Role
Performances

Complex Unstructured
Task Performances

Higher Order Competencies

Structured Task Performances

Discrete Content Skills

High

Low

(Cognitive) (Functional) (Relational) (Language)

From the simple...

The simplest forms of demonstrations or competence are found in the bottom sector of the Mountain. They are the forms that most of the behavioral objectives of yesteryear took: either simple, discrete skills tied to very particular segments of content or tasks that are mainly predefined and prestructured by the teacher — as most schoolwork assignments are. Typical examples include:

> Students will correctly identify and label the major rivers and lakes on a topographical map of the United States.

> Students will correctly describe three characteristics that differentiate mammals from other animals.

> Students will correctly compute the sums and differences of mixed fractions.

> Students will write a three-page, grammatically correct essay summarizing the plot of a major novel.

This connection to, and emphasis on, very specific content and the tight structuring of the performance tasks is characteristic of what have come to be called "traditional outcomes." These forms have taken on this name largely because they reflect the system's time-honored way of defining curriculum and learning around traditional content categories. Hence, this lower sector of the Mountain is often regarded as being "content dominated."

As the words outside the Mountain suggest, these relatively simple forms of learning demonstrations do not generally require the complex integration, synthesis, and application of other learning components to be achieved. Nor are the contexts or situations in which the performing is done very complex. To be successful, students usually have to do no more than engage with content while in their seats in self-contained classrooms.

...to the complex

At the top of the Mountain and at the opposite end of the competence hierarchy are the most complex forms of demonstrating learning. They involve the complex learning demonstrations that people must do to function effectively in their occupational, family, civic, and recreational roles. These performance abilities require that individuals integrate, synthesize, and apply a complex array of content and competence, often in the face of the demanding realities, conditions, and challenges that people encounter in those job and community contexts. For that reason, this upper sector of the Mountain is often regarded as "context dominated." These most complex forms of competence are called "complex role performances" and "life-role functioning." Since 1991, they also have taken on the name "transformational outcomes" because they: 1) totally alter old conceptions of how schools define learning and organize themselves to accomplish it and 2) transcend yesteryear's narrow concept of content-bound behavioral objectives.

While the word "role" is a technical term frequently used by social scientists, it is pertinent here because it denotes a position that individuals hold in social systems — a position that has responsibilities, expectations, and opportunities attached to it that truly matter in the long run and over the long haul. (Being a parent is an excellent example of a role within a family social system.) Roles have significance both for those in the role and for those in the system with them, because their relationship and the responsibilities and expectations associated with it are enduring and have consequences that go beyond just a single performance event. Consequently, a role performance is something that everyone in a social system takes seriously because it directly and indirectly affects everyone.

Growing into the role. To be a successful role performer, individuals must possess deeply internalized performance abilities that allow them to operate across a broad range of situations over extended periods of time. Developing these complex, broadly generalized performance abilities requires years of practice with a diversity of content in a variety of circumstances. It is not something a person accomplishes in a specific course or program. Increasingly, those implementing OBE are defining exit outcomes in terms of these complex kinds of role performance abilities because they see them as the forms of learning that do truly matter for students, their parents, and society in the long run.

A trail between the simple and complex

Lying between what appear to be these two extremes are forms of demonstrations and competence that provide the potential pathway from the bottom to the top of the Mountain. Hence, they have come to be called transitional outcomes. They include a broad range of competencies considered in educational circles as "higher order" — things like effective communication, investigative research, complex analysis, problem solving and decision making, and abilities that go beyond the knowledge and skills inherent in particular subjects.

For that reason, this middle sector of the Mountain is often regarded as "competence dominated." These higher order competencies reflect the learner's ability to do complex things with a broad range of ideas and information, not just single subjects. Consequently, they literally invite staff to step beyond the constraints of individual content areas and take a more interdisciplinary and thematic approach to curriculum design and delivery.

These transitional outcomes also include what are called "complex unstructured task performances" — a long name to be sure, but a very precise description for the ability to use the knowledge and competence represented in the bottom part of the Mountain to invent or create projects, products, or processes on one's own. In other words, at this level of the Mountain the learners are not simply carrying out tasks defined and assigned by others, but are taking the initiative and responsibility to design and create new things without being told exactly what these things must be or how they must look. (This strongly parallels what Theodore Sizer has described as "significant exhibitions of learning" for high school students — exhibitions that require in-depth, original treatment of broad bodies of information, ideas, and competence.) These may take the form of major research projects, inventions, creative works, and significant action projects. And this level is the key stepping stone to learners developing the self-direction and motivation required in the roles and responsibilities they will assume after leaving school.

12. How do these most complex transitional and transformational forms of learning demonstrations relate to traditional measures of school achievement?

The challenge facing schools today is how to bridge the enormous gap between traditional school learning and measures of achievement and the "authentic" and complex demonstrations of competence people have to do once they leave their classroom seats. During the past decade, those implementing OBE have concluded — based on widespread public criticism and data from the world of work — that school learning by itself often doesn't make students competent for what faces them in the real world.

Consequently, educators are being compelled to redefine their conception of schooling outcomes and how to measure them by changing their focus from the bottom sector of the Mountain to the top. This is a huge leap for a system whose definition and measurement of student learning and achievement has almost exclusively focused on pencil and paper testing, scoring, and grading of things at the bottom of the Mountain.

Tests reveal a small portion of what students know and how they can manipulate information mentally. But they usually are inadequate for measuring any of the competencies in the upper sectors of the Mountain that require learners to actually do things with what they know. Complex forms of doing — like organizing, planning, designing, and producing — can only be measured by having students actually organize, plan, design, and produce things and then observing the results of their endeavors.

This kind of measurement is called "authentic performance assessment" because it has students do exactly what the verb and the content require: organize, plan, design, produce, or carry out the demonstration processes embedded in the outcome.

Authentic performance assessment poses a huge dilemma for both educators and the public. Namely, though it is a more precise approach to measuring performances, it is still in its infancy in schools. Its development and adequate implementation, then, are bound to be slow. This leaves schools in a "Catch-22" position. They need to help students develop complex competencies, but they aren't absolutely sure how to measure them. So they continue having students take conventional tests that the public thinks it understands, while knowing that those tests fall decidedly short of measuring the most significant kinds of learning and competence. If a solution to this dilemma is to be found, it must start with a more careful and precise definition of outcomes themselves. The more carefully this is done, the clearer the picture educators will have regarding what to teach, how to teach it, what to assess, and how to assess it.

13. Are there examples of role performance outcomes that districts can use to begin their OBE planning and implementation?

Yes, there are two different types of examples. The first is in the exit outcomes frameworks of several U.S. and Canadian districts. While these district examples vary in terms of their technical formatting and substance, they do reflect a blending of the two kinds of demonstrations in the transformational zone of the Mountain. The following school districts have somewhat similar examples that other districts could study: Aurora, Colorado; College Community Schools in Cedar Rapids, Iowa; Dublin,

Ohio; Flint, Michigan; Fontana, California; Mooresville, North
Carolina; Syracuse, New York; Walled Lake, Michigan: Waterford,
Michigan; Waterloo County, Ontario; and Yarmouth, Maine.

If we were to construct a general composite of the role performance
outcomes these districts have developed, we would find considerable over-
lap among the general types of role performers they identify as essential
for students to become. But they vary considerably in identifying the
qualitative attributes they think those role performers should possess and
exhibit. Listed below are the most common role performer labels used in
district exit outcome frameworks, along with the range of attributes that
has been used to more fully define them.

- LEARNERS (Self-Directed, Continuously Developing,
  Lifelong, Collaborative)

- CITIZENS (Informed, Involved, Global, World,
  Responsible, Accountable, Contributing)

- THINKERS (Perceptive, Constructive, Complex)

- PARTICIPANTS (Creative, Active, Culturally Literate)

- INDIVIDUALS (Dependable, Healthy, Fulfilled, Self-
  Directed, Continuously Developing)

- CONTRIBUTORS (Collaborative, Community, Reflective,
  Expressive, Informed)

- PRODUCERS/WORKERS (Collaborative, Adaptable,
  Quality)

- COMMUNICATORS (Effective, Responsible, Concerned)

- PERSONS (Caring, Accepting, Supportive, Authentic,
  Well-Rounded, Competent, Confident)

In reflecting on these role performer labels and attributes, please note that
they are only that. They are not clearly defined role performances around
which curriculum, instruction, and assessment can all be unambiguously
designed. For that to be the case, the label and its attributes would have to
be "operationalized" — a fancy word for "made tangible" and "put into practice." This requires districts to identify and define the essential performance
components that constitute that particular type of role performer.

A district approach. A particularly expansive example taken from Mooresville, North Carolina's, framework of "High Performance Expectations and Success Skills" is shown below. Among other things, the Mooresville community wants each of its graduates to be a continuously developing, lifelong, self-directed learner who:

- Assumes responsibility for decisions and activities.

- Identifies and applies a set of goals to actions and purposes.

- Articulates and uses a design for continuous improvement.

- Creates, maintains, and enhances a healthy physical, mental, emotional, personal self with a positive image.

- Articulates a vision for learning.

- Initiates and values continuous learning.

- Accesses and analyzes information to reason, communicate, make responsible decisions, and solve problems.

- Applies information and demonstrates abilities to reason, communicate, make responsible decisions, and solve problems in school and real-life situations.

- Uses a scientific approach in solving problems.

A composite approach. The second kind of example reflects a composite of elements found in many of these district frameworks, plus significant studies of workplace requirements in the Information Age. One of the most widely quoted studies is the 1992 SCANS Report. SCANS stands for "Secretary's Commission on Achieving Needed Skills," and the report was commissioned and disseminated by the U.S. Department of Labor. Its recommendations go far beyond the conventions of the academic curriculum, and they have served as the starting point for many state and district reform initiatives, including Florida's widely recognized Blueprint 2000.

Described here is a framework of significant performance roles that parallels these workplace analyses and combines elements from both of the categories in the transformational sector of the Demonstration Mountain — hence, its name: Fundamental Life Performance Roles. The framework is illustrated in Figure 3.6.

FIGURE 3.6

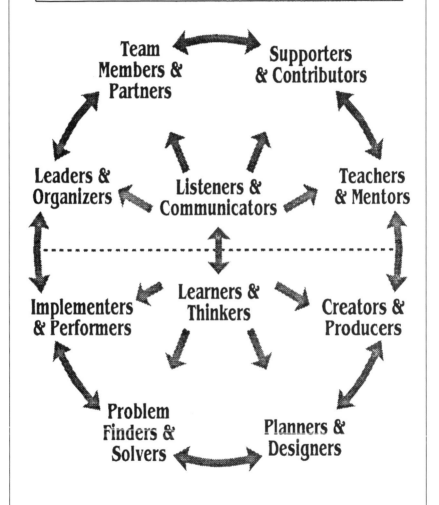

Fundamental Life Performance Roles

The pictorial representation of this comprehensive framework shows that what we have called role performances falls into two broad categories. Above the dotted line are social and interpersonal performance roles that inherently involve interactions with other people. These include:

- **Listeners and Communicators** who can grasp and express ideas, information, intention, feeling, and concern for others in ways that are clearly understood and appreciated.

- **Teachers and Mentors** who can enhance the thinking, skills, performance orientations, and motivation of others through the explanations they provide, the counsel they give, and the example they set.

- **Supporters and Contributors** who invest time, ideas, and resources to improve the quality of life of those around them.

- **Team Members and Partners** who contribute their best efforts to collaborative endeavors and who seek agreement on goals, procedures, responsibilities and rewards, setting aside personal preferences in order to accomplish mutual aims.

- **Leaders and Organizers** who can initiate, coordinate, and facilitate the accomplishment of collective tasks by perceiving and defining intended results, determining how they might be accomplished, anticipating roadblocks, and enlisting and supporting the participation of others to achieve the results.

Below the line are performance roles, inherently more technical and strategic in character — roles that individuals potentially could carry out entirely on their own but that also might involve others. These include:

- **Learners and Thinkers** who develop and use cognitive tools and strategies to translate new information and experiences into sound action. They might use their repertoire of knowledge and strategies to extend their capacities for successful action by assimilating, analyzing, and synthesizing new ideas and experiences.

- **Implementers and Performers** who can apply basic and advanced ideas, information, skills, tools, and technologies as they carry out the responsibilities associated with all life roles.

- **Problem Finders and Solvers** who can anticipate, explore, analyze, and resolve problems by examining their underlying causes from a variety of perspectives and then develop potential solutions to them.

- **Planners and Designers** who can develop effective plans, methods, and strategies for anticipating and resolving issues and problems and for charting new courses of action.

- **Creators and Producers** who seek new possibilities for understanding or doing things and who translate those possibilities into original, workable products or processes that change the working or living environment.

One apparent strength of this framework as a starting point for districts wanting to develop outcomes of significance is that these performance roles are critical components of a variety of life roles. Parenting requires them; occupational roles require them; and effective citizenship requires them.

Another strength is that it explicitly states some key performance roles in what is broadly regarded as "social and leadership skills" — the things above the dotted line that many employers today claim are more essential to effective job performance than some of the technical and strategic competencies below the line.

But a word of caution is in order. These 10 fundamental life performance roles should not be considered fully developed exit outcomes. As in the district examples just described, the figure contains the labels for important performance roles; but these labels are not clearly defined performances in their own right.

To be a fully defined outcome, each of the 10 sets of role performance labels in Figure 3.6 needs to be translated directly into a set of components that embody what that performance role looks like in action. Much like the Mooresville "Learner" example, these components would be even more precisely defined statements than the 10 captions just presented. At a minimum, each performance statement or component links a significant demonstration verb (DO) to a significant body of substance (WHAT) to indicate clearly one of the critical things that type of role performer must do to be successful. These "operational" components provide the real guide to what must be taught, learned, assessed, and reported.

14. Is it realistic for schools to prepare students to become successful at complex role performances?

Yes, but five major things have to happen in order for them to succeed:

1) The stakeholders in districts will have to agree that role performance abilities like those in Figure 3.6 are what they want for their students. Without strong support for a well-defined outcome framework of this kind, this expectation is not realistic.

2) The system's traditional conception of curriculum will have to expand dramatically from a preoccupation with short-term content learning to a shared emphasis on the continuous strengthening of students' abilities to do meaningful things with content and to relate to each other. Implementation assistance in transformational OBE approaches already is helping districts move in this direction.

3) The nature of instructional practice will have to involve an active learning approach with students continuously carrying out performance roles. Along with their learning and performance team members, students must engage in increasingly complex content. Extensive team-based learning projects will be a must if students are to develop the interpersonal and communication abilities required in the Information Age world of work. Prototypes for how this can be done already exist and are being used and refined by teachers at all grade levels.

4) The range of settings in which students learn and demonstrate their learning will have to be expanded considerably because the four walls of the classroom and what individual teachers can model and teach will be too limiting for what is required of students. At a minimum, this context expansion will allow students a great deal more engagement with experts and organizations in the larger community, leading to a redefinition of who is a teacher and what is an appropriate setting for learning.

5) The focus and effectiveness of both preservice and inservice programs for teachers will have to expand far beyond their current parameters because it is extremely unlikely teachers will be able to assist students with things they themselves cannot do effectively. This implies that the performance role framework in Figure 3.6 could serve as a template for professional training as well as for student exit outcomes.

15. How have districts typically determined what their major outcomes for students should be?

Historically, districts have used four methods to determine their major outcomes. But during the past several years, use of one of those approaches has sharply decreased: one in which individual teachers were encouraged to develop their own outcomes for their own classes. While this method was seen as a useful strategy to help teachers get started and take ownership of their OBE work, the need for a common purpose and focus across classrooms and schools became very apparent to local educators and policymakers. Consequently, almost all current OBE design efforts involve large numbers of people determining the desired outcomes for the district as a whole, for individual programs, or for both.

Content Experts. Of the three most prevalent methods being used today, the content expert approach has the longest history. It typically involves teams of teachers and curriculum experts conducting thorough analyses of the various subject areas in the curriculum and determining, often by using models from national professional associations, what is most important in those fields for students to learn. In simplified form, the driving question that guides this process is: "What should they know?" The result is usually a framework of knowledge and skills focused on developing students' subject matter expertise. The term commonly applied to the results of this approach is "program outcomes" because the outcomes developed are usually program specific, for math, social studies, and so forth. In addition, the outcomes that result from this process fall almost exclusively in the bottom half of the Demonstration Mountain. They are structured task performances and competencies tied to specific subject area content.

Community Consensus. This approach, often the most eclectic, uses a variety of strategies for enlisting input from both staff and community members. As its name implies, this approach goes well beyond the education community to seek input about district-level outcomes. For both political and substantive reasons, it enlists some form of either direct participation or representation of virtually all of the apparent stakeholder groups in a community, including teachers and administrators. As the name also implies, the result of this process is an agreement, sometimes implicit and sometimes quite explicit, regarding what will be endorsed in policy as the exit outcomes for the district.

The simplified form of the question that usually guides this process is: "What should students be able to do?" Sometimes participants are simply asked to state their personal preferences and a consensus process works out the differences. In other versions, people are asked to examine data about labor market trends and changes in society and then offer their opinions. The usual result of this approach is an exit outcomes framework that includes predominantly higher order competencies, which fall within the transitional sector of the Demonstration Mountain and cut across all study areas.

Context Analysis. The third prevalent method, the context analysis approach, parallels the community consensus approach in its emphasis on directly involving as many community people, educators, and students as possible. It differs in that all of these individuals participate in a much more extensive and tightly designed process called strategic design, in which they:

1) Develop a framework that identifies the significant dimensions and arenas of living in which students will need to be successful following their schooling experience.

2) Determine, by examining a broad range of research on the future, the major challenges and conditions that students are likely to encounter in each of those arenas.

3) Derive directly from the prior two steps a framework of role performance exit outcomes that clearly reflect the civic values the community explicitly endorses and that fall within the transformational sector of the Mountain.

In its simplified form, the key question that drives this strategic design process is: "What will students face?" Each of the districts mentioned in response to question 13 has gone through some version of this process.

It is possible, of course, for districts to use amalgamations of all three processes to determine their major outcomes, but our experience suggests that most of these derivations closely resemble the community consensus approach. They involve more than just school staff, ask participants to look generally at the future, and focus on what students should know and be able to do in both school and beyond. The result is a combination of what we have called traditional and transitional outcomes.

16. How does this strategic design process differ from common forms of strategic planning?

Districts seriously interested in implementing OBE should probably do both strategic design and strategic planning, but in a definite order and with a clear purpose for making the connection. General forms of strategic planning have districts define their mission, values, and needs and, from there, develop a comprehensive set of program and logistical priorities and action plans to specifically address them. These priorities and plans might or might not have anything to do with student outcomes or OBE.

Strategic design also has districts determine their mission and values, but with the explicit intent of using them as guides to develop a framework of future-grounded exit outcomes. For any district serious about implementing OBE, strategic design should come first because their exit outcomes need to serve as the driving force for whatever implementation planning follows. Some districts recently have begun to follow their outcome derivation process by engaging in "Outcome-Based Action Planning," a process developed by Charles Schwahn, a key consultant with the High Success Network. Schwahn's process resembles strategic planning but uses the district's exit outcome framework and OBE's purposes and principles to: 1) focus and align all of the district's programmatic and logistical priorities and plans and 2) drive the strategic decisions necessary for assuring that OBE implementation will be successful. The process explicitly addresses 20 key dimensions of a district's operational and support systems and documents stages of implementation readiness and progress on each of them.

17. How can we be sure a district will define outcomes that will truly matter for students beyond their schooling experience?

There are no guarantees, but the strategic design process just described was developed to assist districts in establishing the strongest possible connection between the conditions students are likely to face in the near future and what they will need to know, do, and be like in order to deal with those conditions successfully. To many people, this seems like a sounder approach than building the outcomes strictly from static subject matter frameworks or from personal opinions and preferences. Given the rapid pace of change today, districts planning to engage in some form of future-focused strategic design should repeat the process every few years since exit outcomes need to be continually refined to match emerging future trends.

Summary

What are the most important things to remember about what outcomes are and how they are derived? As we develop a clearer picture of OBE implementation in later chapters, it's important to keep in mind these seven key things about outcomes:

1) Outcomes are the actual results of learning that students visibly demonstrate. They involve the integration and application of content, competence, and confidence in actual performance settings when or after formal instructional experiences are over.

2) Values, attitudes, psychological states of mind, scores, and averages are not outcomes and should not be represented as such.

3) Since outcomes vary enormously in their focus, content, complexity, and significance, districts should be explicit about both the performance capabilities they want to ensure for their students and the literacy and content outcomes underlying those performance abilities.

4) In general, the more outcomes reflect actual role performances, the more they will directly support students' success
after leaving school — but the more traditional schooling
practices will have to change to achieve them.

5) Frameworks of role performance exit outcomes that districts
can use as guides for their own outcome development
process exist, linked to the demands of the Information Age
world and marketplace.

6) To have both political legitimacy and a focus on students'
futures, district outcome derivation processes must have the
most extensive community input possible.

7) The strategic design process gives districts the strongest possible rationale for developing exit outcomes that will benefit
their students directly after they leave school, as well as for
designing and carrying out strategic action planning that
directly supports the accomplishment of the outcomes.

Chapter 4
What Are the Major Trends in Outcome-Based Implementation?

The first three chapters have clearly indicated that both outcomes and their implementation take different forms. In fact, the range of these forms is almost as diverse as the number of states, districts, and schools involved because there are so many different ways that OBE's paradigm, purposes, and principles can be applied to a wide variety of outcome frameworks. Nonetheless, commonalities among these initiatives can be found and organized around four major configurations of practice: classroom reform, program alignment, external accountability, and system transformation.

These configurations, or what we will call "Faces of OBE," are composed of the four major frameworks established earlier in the book. By using these four frameworks to cluster, organize, and interpret what is happening in the field, we can establish a middle ground between OBE appearing to mean and be just one thing, and OBE appearing to mean and be anything that happens to go by that name in a given state, district, or school. We will discover in this chapter that the four major faces of OBE continue to evolve in important ways over time.

Culminating outcomes. The first framework used to distinguish among these various patterns of OBE practice is the Demonstration Mountain presented in Figure 3.5 of Chapter 3. The Mountain is fundamental to understanding and mapping models of OBE because the nature of any implementation effort is going to be strongly influenced by what the system defines as its culminating outcomes. This relates not only to the content and interconnectedness of outcomes, but to their forms as well. The forms that learning demonstrations take vary greatly from micro to macro and from simple to complex dimensions; both types directly affect curriculum design, instructional delivery, time use and structuring, assessment designs, and credentialing practices.

Operational structures. The second framework needed for understanding and mapping models of OBE was presented in Figure 1.8 near the end of Chapter 1. It involves what we called the operational structures of the system — those fundamental patterns of programmatic operations that define and shape what happens in a school and its classrooms on a regular basis. We named them the standards and accountability structure, the curriculum content and articulation structure, the instructional process and technology structure, and the eligibility and assignment structure. This framework is essential in describing and classifying approaches to OBE because it represents the heart of how schools and districts are organized and operate.

Institutional level. The third framework we will call the institutional level of the K-12 system's operations. In the educational world those key organizational levels range from the classroom as the most micro-level to the department, school, district, state, and suprastate levels. The latter refers to a combination of institutions, agencies, and organizations that strongly influence how education is carried out, but have varying degrees of formal jurisdiction over the K-12 system. Regional accreditation agencies, colleges and universities, federal programs, publishing and testing companies, and national professional associations are all examples.

Purposes and principles. The fourth cuts across the other three interlocking frameworks: the purposes and principles of OBE. In other words, the forces discussed in Chapter 1 that make OBE what it is and distinguish it as fundamentally different from the time-based, Industrial Age features of our current system.

So, the overall framework developed and used in this chapter assumes that any given example of OBE implementation will reflect 1) how OBE's two purposes and four principles shape 2) the system's four key operational functions, 3) at which institutional levels, 4) in pursuit of which kind of culminating outcomes. To fully develop and map this analysis in detail requires a four-dimensional matrix that is beyond the scope of this book. Instead, we will address each of these four critical dimensions through basic questions that arise around each of four broad faces of OBE practice that encompass most of what is being called OBE in the field today.

1. What are the key configurations of OBE in today's school reform efforts?

To some extent the four faces of OBE parallel the micro to macro evolution of OBE thinking and practice over the past two decades (described near the end of Chapter 1). It is useful to think of these four faces as:

Classroom Reform

Program Alignment

External Accountability

System Transformation

Each configuration has a distinctive focus, character, and agenda for changing and reforming our traditional system of schooling.

2. What are some of the key characteristics of the classroom reform approach to OBE?

This face of OBE has the longest history and the narrowest scope of any of the four configurations. It emerged in the late '60s and early '70s in the writings of Benjamin Bloom (1968) and James Block (1971). From 1968 well into the 1970s, the picture in Figure 4.1 (see page 82) represented the entirety of what we know today as OBE. Its level of institutional focus is mainly the individual classroom, and the understanding and application of OBE's purposes and principles follows that same intra-classroom approach to reforming instructional processes and delivery structures. Known widely as "Mastery Learning," this classroom reform face of OBE has lengthy literature on its design, implementation, and effectiveness, summarized in the 1989 book *Building Effective Mastery Learning Schools* by Block, Helen Efthim, and Robert Burns.

Listed below are some of the key characteristics of the classroom reform approach:

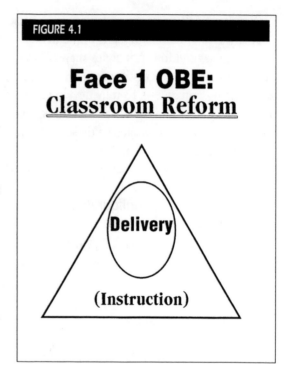

FIGURE 4.1

Face 1 OBE:
Classroom Reform

Delivery

(Instruction)

Institutional Level

Mainly self-contained classrooms; some departmental or grade-level teaming.

Culminating Outcomes

Almost entirely discrete content skills and structured task performances from the traditional sector of the Mountain, defined as lesson and unit outcomes for segments of particular content areas — a totally micro-focus on successful learning and achievement.

Standards and Accountability Structure

Sets higher acceptability and passing standards than does the traditional system. Leaves achievement measures, testing, grading, and reporting largely unchanged except for consistent use of "second chances" on tests and assignments.

Curriculum Content and Articulation Structure

Better focusing of curriculum priorities and prerequisites for learning success within the classroom, but overall curriculum content and structure are generally unchanged from the traditional system. Existing curriculum is the prevalent basis for defining outcomes.

Instructional Process and Technology Structure

Major attention paid to consistently applying the clarity of focus, expanded opportunity, and high expectations principles to lessons and units as they occur. Both corrective and extension and enrichment experiences offered to students after initial instruction and testing. Serious attempt to create classroom climate of success. Students often work in learning teams and help each other learn.

Eligibility and Assignment Structure

Assumes self-contained classroom situation with the same group of students for nine months on the same fixed schedule. Some teachers voluntarily team and create time and grouping flexibilities. Attempts made to eliminate permanent ability groups and enable all students to advance to high-challenge curriculum. Some "continuous progress" models established in elementary schools, but whole-class strategies prevail.

The Four Principles

Applied with a strong micro-focus on culminating outcomes, time and opportunity, and curriculum design. Everything implemented in terms of accomplishing small, finite segments of learning within traditional time schedules.

Two things stand out about this classroom reform face of OBE. First, as strongly intimated earlier, it has always focused on what teachers as empowered individuals could do to improve the conditions of opportunity and learning in their own classrooms, regardless of the constraints of the current system's calendar, schedule, curriculum, grading and reporting system, school structure, and teachers' contract, among others. In doing so, it centered on the teacher as the key agent of OBE reform.

Second, its definition of learning success is grounded on the objectives that individual teachers can identify and address within the content and curriculum segments they are assigned to teach. Therefore, it has brought about instructional improvement and increased student success by applying OBE's purposes and principles to the instructional process in all content areas, grade levels, and kinds of schools.

3. What are some of the key strengths and limitations of the classroom reform approach?

The strengths of the classroom reform approach are twofold:

1) It focuses on what teachers themselves can do to improve instructional effectiveness and student learning, given the organizational and time realities that most of them face. There is ample evidence that this approach's impact has been considerable over the years.

2) It points out that there is far more learning potential in most students than is tapped by the time-based, Industrial Age paradigm. Just a little clarity of focus, expanded opportunity, and high expectations at the classroom level can go a long way toward fostering increased student learning and motivation.

The classroom reform approach's limitations also are clear:

1) It does not address the larger outcomes, curriculum, assessment, credentialing, organizational, and policy issues vital to fully developing an OBE system. Hence, it leaves the constraints of the time-based paradigm described in Chapter 2 largely unaddressed.

2) Its focus on the key factors listed above is inherently micro: micro-outcomes, micro-curriculum segments, micro-focus on time and opportunity, and so forth. This may reflect a pattern of learning improvement taking place on a day-to-day basis that does not translate to students having more success on complex performances in more complex performance situations. Expanding each of these components in a more macro-direction takes systemwide staff involvement far beyond the jurisdiction, expertise, and influence of the individual teacher.

4. What are some of the key characteristics of the program alignment approach to OBE?

This second face of OBE has become the most prevalent and diverse in the field. Early forms of it arose in the mid-1970s as a way of extending Mastery Learning and its classroom reform focus beyond the individual classroom. Over time it has become a standard among districts seeking to improve their performance on a variety of curriculum and competence outcomes. As suggested by the diagram in Figure 4.2, the dominant agenda of the program alignment approach is design that attempts to bring the core content of a school's or district's curriculum and instruction components into tight congruence with each other and with declared culminating outcomes. The aim is to enhance the impact of the classroom reform model by establishing clarity of focus, consistency, and continuity in all aspects of curriculum and instruction within and across a school's classrooms and a district's schools. That commonality of focus and content clearly assists students as they move from class to class throughout their school careers.

Listed below are some of the key characteristics of the program alignment approach:

Institutional Level

Ranges from departments or grade levels in buildings through all programs and schools within a district. Most newer examples address the total district curriculum.

Culminating Outcomes

Range greatly from site to site. Some defined as course outcomes, others as program outcomes, still others as exit outcomes. Usually mixtures of discrete content skills, structured task performances,

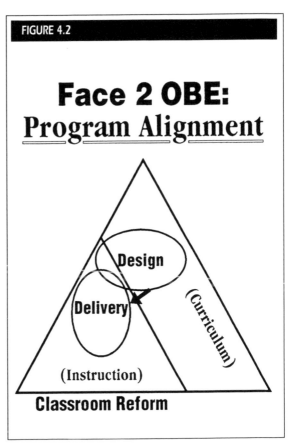

FIGURE 4.2

Face 2 OBE:
Program Alignment

Design

Delivery

(Curriculum)

(Instruction)

Classroom Reform

and higher order competencies from the traditional and transitional sectors of the Mountain. Evolving trend toward using complex unstructured task performance projects from the transitional sector of the Mountain as graduation requirements for high school seniors.

Standards and Accountability Structure

Sets clearer and higher acceptability and passing standards than does the traditional system. Most achievement measures, assessments, grading, and reporting are largely unchanged from the existing system except for a strong trend toward 1) using authentic assessments, program and/or exit outcomes; 2) using A,B,I grading (which treats B as the minimum performance expectation and passing grade); and 3) basing grades and credit on end-of-year, rather than on averaged performances. Consistent use of "second or multiple chances" on tests and assignments.

Curriculum Content and Articulation Structure

Highly variable across districts, depending on whether they have an exit outcome framework that is more than traditional content-focused demonstrations. Serious attempts at getting content to match and support outcomes and getting grade levels and courses to connect more closely. Clear attempts across the grade levels at creating interdisciplinary units, courses, and programs in pursuit of outcomes from the transitional sector of the Mountain.

Instructional Process and Technology Structure

Enormous variability depending on the existence and nature of the district's culminating outcomes. Culminating outcomes from the traditional sector of the Mountain encourage continued use of conventional instructional delivery practices. Exit outcomes from the transitional sector challenge conventional, single-subject curriculum designs, teaching strategies, and assessment and grading practices. Often old practices don't match the new outcomes, but public reaction demands that they be continued — especially testing and grading. Major attention paid to consistently applying the four principles to units and courses. Limited attempts to apply them at the macro-culminating levels (program and exit outcomes). Serious attempts to create district, school, and classroom climates of success. Students often work in same-class learning teams to help each other learn and to get feedback on outcome performances. Some cross-age learning teams and tutoring being instituted.

Eligibility and Assignment Structure

Increasing evidence of teacher teaming, both within and across grade levels, and across subject areas in high schools. Major trend toward block scheduling and using time, personnel, and resources more effectively in support of student learning success. Clear evidence of attempts to eliminate low-level courses, programs, and ability groups from schools. Access to high-challenge curriculum definitely increasing K-12. Use of computer-assisted instruction is fostering "continuous progress" models in basic skills development in all grades.

The Four Principles

Applied with a strong focus on unit and course culminating outcomes, time and opportunity, and curriculum design. More macro-level applications still developing. Major challenge is how to expand implementation beyond constraints of natural calendar year to make program and exit outcomes "real."

Matchmaking. The term "alignment" basically means "perfect match." This largely district-level approach to OBE attempts to get four things to match, so that the application of OBE's two purposes and four principles will be enhanced: 1) what's important for students to learn, 2) what we're teaching them, 3) how we're teaching them, and 4) what we're assessing when we ask them to perform. The harsh reality that most districts face when they engage in this alignment approach to design is that mismatches and gaps occur everywhere. From a common-sense perspective, alignment is bound to improve the consistency and effectiveness of the overall program. The consistent application of the four principles enhances it further.

There are two major trends in how this approach has been pursued. Starting in the '70s and continuing to the present is what some call the "CBO approach." CBO stands for curriculum-based outcomes, content-bound objectives, and calendar-based organization. In other words, educators started with the curriculum and program structures they already had and developed unit, course, and eventually program outcomes and an alignment process for them. This closely parallels the content expert approach to deriving outcomes that was discussed in the latter part of Chapter 3. Added to this are the very real pressures to have the curriculum and the outcomes perfectly match what students will face on state or national tests — which leads to TBO (testing-based outcomes) driving CBO, but calling both "OBE." With 20-20 hindsight and a purist perspective, it's easy to see how this early approach to program alignment is a bit like having the tail wag the dog.

A growing trend. During the past several years, however, the program alignment approach has evolved appreciably, largely as the result of exit outcomes emerging as a major factor in the design and implementation thinking of districts new to OBE. What was initially an exclusive focus on the unique content of each program area evolved gradually into an awareness that all programs need to align with the thrust of the district's overall exit outcomes. As this recognition occurred, the outcomes in the transitional and transformational sectors of the Demonstration Mountain have become increasingly more central in district curriculum designs.

Many districts and some states have come to realize that the curriculum should be aligned around their culminating outcomes of significance for students, rather than using the existing curriculum to write traditional sector content outcomes. Because of this change in thinking about the connection between outcomes and the curriculum, districts that have adopted OBE more recently have been able to avoid some of the historical shortcomings of the CBO and TBO approaches to program alignment.

5. What are some of the key strengths and limitations of the curriculum alignment approach?

The curriculum alignment approach to OBE has at least four key strengths:

1) It expands the OBE agenda well beyond individual classrooms and engages all instructional staff in systematically examining what, why, and how they are doing what they are doing, and how it relates to significant student learning priorities.

2) This "realignment" allows districts to fill in gaps and eliminate redundancies in their instructional programs across the board, based on clearly defined priorities.

3) It compels staff to examine what, why, and how they are assessing and reporting student learning, and to make the assessment and credentialing system consistent with their curriculum and culminating outcomes.

4) It fosters collaboration among staff: within and across grade levels, within and across subjects, and within and across buildings.

As already mentioned, the key drawback to this approach is that most early efforts simply took the curriculum, delivery, time, and organizational structures of the traditional Industrial Age paradigm as "givens" and treated them as inevitable and unchangeable features of schooling. The key issue for those implementing this approach is whether those structures should serve as the basis for determining student outcomes (CBO) or whether needed outcomes should be the basis for redirecting, redefining, and realigning those prevalent structures (OBE). The purpose served by the classroom reform and program alignment approaches has primarily been to improve and make the existing system more effective — which it has done. The other choice, to be explored shortly, is to use powerful outcomes of significance and OBE to fundamentally "transform" the system.

6. What are some of the key characteristics of the external accountability approach to OBE?

For many reasons, this third face of OBE is its most problematic. Its emphasis on external accountability and the reactions, both within and outside the system, to that increase in governmentally controlled accountability have generated countless headlines and major political controversies

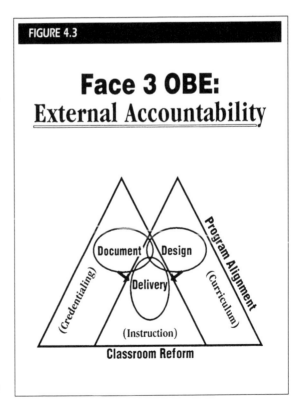

FIGURE 4.3

Face 3 OBE:
External Accountability

since 1992. As suggested by the diagram in Figure 4.3, this approach adds a significant, asymmetric dimension to the OBE picture — a dimension that involves the state-legislated demand for better results and clearer documentation of actual student learning from the system. These new demands directly affect performance standards, graduation requirements, the credentialing of student learning and achievement, and the accreditation of schools.

At the heart of this approach are the actions taken primarily by state policymaking bodies to alter the framework of standards that define and affect 1) what students must do to get promoted within and ultimately to graduate from school with an approved diploma and 2) what schools must do to assure continued accreditation. For some time, these policy groups have been disillusioned with the apparent lack of accuracy, validity, and reliability of teacher grades and Carnegie units of credit in portraying both what students have learned and can do as qualifications for promotion and graduation, and with what serve as valid indicators of educational quality. What these state board members and legislators want instead is better documentation of what students can clearly demonstrate. This will provide the public and the consumers of the educational system with convincing evidence that students are prepared for the challenges that await them beyond the schoolhouse door and also that schools are working.

Therefore, several states have been demanding that documentation of actual student learning be added to grades and credits as a key part of the graduation equation. In some cases, they are requiring students to perform at certain levels on existing standardized tests. In others, states have developed specific outcome frameworks for districts and their students to use as minimum conditions for graduation. The message to the field and the public is:

> Districts and students are accountable for achieving at least a defined set of results or the state will not endorse their programs and credentials.

Listed below are some of the key characteristics of the external accountability approach based on the frameworks discussed at the beginning of this chapter:

Institutional Level

Emanates from various state bodies and has direct impact on districts, their schools, and their students.

Culminating Outcomes

Range greatly from state to state. Some have none, only testing requirements. Many have mixtures of discrete content skills, structured task performances, and higher order competencies from the traditional and transitional sectors of the Mountain, which are equivalent to program and/or exit outcomes. A few have outcome frameworks primarily reflecting the Mountain's transitional and transformational sectors. The latitude given to districts in designing and implementing these state outcomes varies greatly. In a few cases, the legislated consequences of either noncompliance or failure to improve are severe.

Standards and Accountability Structure

Clear intent to supplement, if not replace, conventional grading and course credit standards for graduation. If not clearer, then at least higher standards than current minimums. Many designing new assessment systems; others giving local districts discretion to design them within guidelines. Testing and grading practices in existing courses largely unaffected, but relegated to lower importance as the key determiner of graduation status. Dates for key "high stakes" performances vary greatly, as do student and district consequences for not meeting standards.

Curriculum Content and Articulation Structure

Potential impact on local districts highly variable, depending on the nature of the state's culminating outcome framework. Traditional frameworks may mean small changes in content but big changes in effectiveness. Transitional and transformational frameworks imply and invite major changes along both dimensions for which few prototypes exist. States and districts will have to invent them.

Instructional Process and Technology Structure

Far greater effectiveness and diversity of approaches implied in almost all state models. Some outcome frameworks directly require use of particular technologies and approaches. Most states silent about how districts and schools are to accomplish the new outcomes or standards.

Enormous variability possible depending on the existence and nature of the state's proposed culminating outcomes. Traditional sector outcomes encourage continued use of conventional instructional delivery practices. Transitional/transformational sector outcomes present unique challenges to conventional curriculum delivery and teaching strategies — expanding possibilities for more contact with outside experts and use of out-of-school learning settings.

Eligibility and Assignment Structure

Very diverse implications regarding structuring of schools, grouping and advancing students, and structuring of time and opportunities. Clear implications in most states that 1) advancement and graduation should be performance-based — not determined by age and time spent in school and 2) all students should emerge as successful. Few states seem to address the inherent dilemma between a time-based system and outcome-based standards.

The Four Principles

Little acknowledgment or evidence in most states that they even exist or are the vital forces in successful OBE implementation. If they are to come into play, local districts will have to learn about and implement them.

7. What are some of the key strengths and limitations of this external accountability approach?

Since state initiatives differ so much, drawing generalizations about strengths and limitations is difficult. Nonetheless, two benefits do stand out:

1) Policymakers across the country are on record endorsing some form of outcomes or performances as the new basis for defining student achievement and establishing graduation standards. "Business as usual" is under siege, and local districts are now compelled to break the institutional inertia of the past and focus on achieving stronger learning results for all their students. In most cases, this emphasis on outcomes directly implies that changes in curriculum content and instructional strategies are imperative.

2) For better and for worse, the terms "outcomes" and "Outcome-Based Education" have become household words

almost overnight — something that OBE advocates and implementers would not have imagined before 1993. The entire discourse regarding school reform has shifted from the traditional emphasis on programs, curriculum, teaching, resources, and procedures to achievement, performance, learning, results, and outcomes.

The three major drawbacks of these state initiatives are just as obvious and represent a formidable obstacle to more authentic forms of local OBE implementation:

1) Too many state initiatives carry the OBE label without embodying its paradigm, purposes, premises, and principles. Instead, they continue to embody most of the features of the traditional education paradigm — only with "outcomes sprinkled on top." By identifying OBE with this third face, both educators and the public are carrying distorted notions of what OBE actually is. These widespread misunderstandings and distortions could diminish the likelihood of authentic OBE implementation occurring on a broad scale in the near future.

2) The mandates of many state initiatives have set off an intense political reaction, which has seriously damaged many promising state and local implementation efforts. These mandates focus on performance accountability without appreciating either what outcomes actually are, what authentic implementation requires, or how to establish the conditions and incentives that local districts need for successfully pursuing and implementing authentic OBE.

3) The technical adequacy of many of these state initiatives and outcome frameworks is highly questionable and has unnecessarily fueled the fire of resistance even further. Because being outcome-based seems like common sense and sounds easy, many states have developed their own frameworks and plans without adequately examining the state-of-the-art in the field. This often sends local districts down unproductive paths and makes even neutral observers cautious about endorsing or supporting what is represented as "OBE."

8. What are some of the key characteristics of the system transformation approach to OBE?

This fourth face of OBE emerged on the scene in the early 1990s as a result of continuing evolution of OBE thinking and practice. The key characteristics of this face include:

1) A future-focused strategic design process that generates a framework of district exit outcomes, which fall into the transformational sector of the Demonstration Mountain. These outcomes reflect the role performance capabilities students will need in facing the challenges and conditions likely to characterize life in the Information Age.

2) Curriculum, instruction, and assessment and credentialing designs directly based on and designed around this exit outcome framework. These designs encourage students to develop and demonstrate complex role performance abilities in all areas of learning and at all stages of their school careers.

3) Heavy emphasis on the use of authentic life contexts, settings, and experiences. They are viewed as both necessary places where learning should occur and realistic settings in which performances should be carried out.

4) A macro-approach to implementing OBE's four principles that uses the district's exit outcomes as the foundation for applying clarity of focus, expanded opportunity, high expectations, and design down.

Figure 4.4 provides a diagram of how this face of OBE sets the direction for the entire system and how the framework of future-focused exit outcomes drives the system's design, delivery, and documentation functions. It also reveals the difference between an authentic, fully developed OBE approach in which outcomes drive curriculum, instruction, and credentialing, and the partial OBE approaches (noted as "obe") in which curriculum and testing frameworks determine the outcomes. This "little obe" designation applies to the classroom reform, program alignment, and external accountability faces just described.

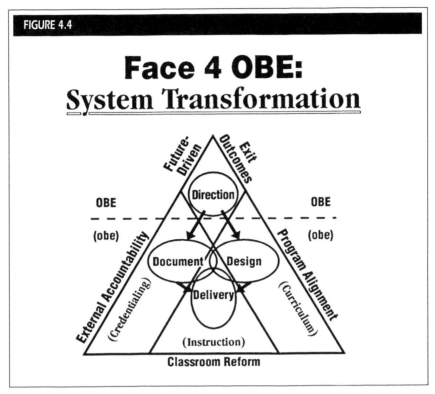

FIGURE 4.4

Face 4 OBE:
System Transformation

Future-Driven

Exit Outcomes

Direction

OBE

OBE

(obe)

(obe)

External Accountability

Program Alignment

Document   Design

(Credentialing)

(Curriculum)

Delivery

(Instruction)

Classroom Reform

Listed below are some of the key characteristics of the system transformation approach:

Institutional Level

Essentially a district approach but, with great care, states and their districts can use it.

Culminating Outcomes

Almost exclusively, exit outcomes are represented in the transformational sector of the Mountain. They are derived through active participation of stakeholder groups in a rigorous analysis of likely future conditions and challenges facing students in the major arenas of living. Many frameworks resemble Figure 3.6 in Chapter 3.

Standards and Accountability Structure

Definite intent to redefine performance and standards around clear criteria and to provide regular reports on actual student learning levels in all key outcome areas. These criteria would replace conventional grading and course credit standards for promotion and graduation. Both clearer and higher standards linked directly to transitional and transformational outcomes. Districts beginning to design authentic assessments and continuously "updatable" performance portfolios and reporting systems for culminating outcomes and their key enablers.

Curriculum Content and Articulation Structure

Opens door to total redirection and redesign of future-focused curriculum, with a problem- and issue-based content focus and continuous development of student abilities along all major competence dimensions. Interdisciplinary and total K-12 planning a must. Designs focus on continuously bringing key culminating outcomes into the classroom at developmentally appropriate levels for students, while fostering mastery of key enabling content and competencies. Far fewer predefined nine-month courses. All students eligible to pursue high-challenge curriculum. Some prototypes are under development.

Instructional Process and Technology Structure

Transitional/transformational outcomes present unique challenges to conventional curriculum delivery and teaching strategies. They open doors to "high engagement/high activity" classrooms staffed by a variety of internal and external experts with continuous emphasis on multimodality active learning by individuals and learning teams. They also foster service learning strategies; learning and performing in authentic, real-world settings; and extensive use of high technology tools and applications. Far less traditional testing and grading done in lieu of more authentic, criterion-based performing, assessing, and reporting.

Eligibility and Assignment Structure

Opens up major new possibilities for structuring schools and instructional delivery systems, grouping and advancing students, and structuring time and opportunities. Extensive teaming of staff with each other and outside experts. More use of focused learning and resource centers. Fewer permanent teacher-student assignment patterns based on fixed schedules. Expanded access to facilities, materials, and learning resources.

The Four Principles

Total commitment to the spirit and letter of the two purposes and four principles — understood and applied by all staff. Clarity of focus on the district's transformational exit outcomes drives the interpretation and application of all four principles.

9. What are some of the key strengths and limitations of the system transformation approach?

There are at least five major strengths of this system transformation face of OBE:

1) It is both future-focused and tightly grounded around a comprehensive framework of key life dimensions—giving it a direct link to the real world.

2) That strong focus on meeting life challenges makes both its outcomes and the curriculum needed to accomplish them highly relevant to students, their families, and future employers. This enhances involvement in the learning process by all parties.

3) The outcome frameworks generated through the strategic design process generally require more complex, significant, and long-lasting learning demonstrations by students than do traditional academic assignments and tests.

4) The emphasis on authentic learning in authentic contexts creates a strong connection among schools, their communities, and outside experts, which enhances communication and trust with those needed most to support school reform and restructuring.

5) The system's framework of role performance exit outcomes encourages a total rethinking of appropriate instructional methods and useful learning and demonstration contexts for students. Passive listening and traditional seat work give way to active and challenging learning environments.

Two key limitations of the system transformation approach in its current form are:

1) Because it represents such a dramatic departure from the thinking, vocabulary, and practices of the all-pervasive and totally familiar time-based Industrial Age paradigm of schooling (described in Figure 2.1 of Chapter 2), this OBE face is hard for many parents and educators to grasp readily.

Consequently, OBE becomes an easy target of criticism for being "new" or "unproven," even though numerous examples exist outside of schools (Figure 1.1 in Chapter 1). Serious examples of district implementation also are emerging throughout North America (see Chapter 5 for details).

OBE becomes an easy target of criticism for being "new" or "unproven," even though numerous examples exist outside of schools. .

2) Precisely because it has not been fully realized in practice by local districts, this approach represents an enormous challenge to states and districts persuaded by its logic, potential, philosophy, and processes. They, along with their more traditionally oriented colleagues, face the challenge of creating schooling anew in the face of serious contradictory pressures: present-day social and labor market realities demanding widespread change confronting a century of institutional inertia resisting it. Reinventing schooling is something that Americans haven't had much practice doing for the past century.

10. Is it really wise to apply the term "OBE" to all four of these major approaches?

The answer to this question may have nothing to do with wisdom or prudence. The fact is that virtually anything having to do with any one of these four approaches is being called OBE by educators, the press, the public, and critics of OBE — without permission and without regard to the major distinctions among them, which we have carefully identified. All four faces are being confused with each other, regardless of their differences.

For those who care about these differences and want to use them to guide future OBE planning and implementation, the answer is "probably not." Using the criteria established in Chapter 1 and the discussion throughout this chapter, we can conclude that the classroom reform approach is not truly OUTCOME-Based in the systemic sense. It is a micro-form of OBE operating in a calendar-based organization/curriculum-based outcomes (CBO) system. The same is true for most of the existing examples and applications of the program alignment and external accountability models. For the most part, they have started with the curriculum, calendar, and organizational structures of schools as givens (CBO) and have done their best to introduce outcomes and OBE's purposes, premises, and principles into that organizational mix. The result, as Figure 4.4 suggests, is more like "(obe)" than "OBE."

The system transformation approach then, is the one face of OBE that:

1) Actually starts with culminating outcomes of significance and bases everything else on them.

2) Consistently makes WHAT and WHETHER more important than WHEN and HOW.

3) Applies OBE's purposes, premises, and principles to their fullest measure.

Without question, this approach represents a challenging ideal for states and districts to emulate and implement, but it is what OBE really means when viewed logically and systemically.

11. Can districts evolve from a classroom reform approach to a system transformation approach over time?

Possibly, but it would require great and continuous change. Any district wanting to begin OBE implementation today should start with some form of the program alignment approach. From the beginning, they could be working toward a common set of program or exit outcomes with at least a foothold in the transitional sector of the Mountain. Without being guided by a common direction and purpose at least that high on the Mountain, teachers will find it difficult to move beyond the familiar surroundings and constraints of the traditional, content-focused sector. And the longer they remain in that content-dominated sector, the more difficult it will become to define learning in more complex performance terms and to teach students how to demonstrate those more complex forms of learning.

Getting to the transformational peak of the Mountain is much easier if you know it's there and are guided by the outcomes in that sector, even if you know that the climb is going to take awhile. Staff who are fast climbers can explore feasible routes to the top. Once traveled enough, those routes will be familiar and safe enough for everyone to take. But if no one is ever encouraged to venture beyond the foothills, the Mountain will always look dangerous, foreboding, or impossible.

12. Is it possible for individual schools to be outcome based without involving the total district?

Like many reform ideas, OBE "evolved up" from the classroom to the building, district, state, and beyond. Because of this history, individual schools have stood out as pioneers and models for others to follow. These schools usually had exceptional principals and teachers and a superintendent and board that gave them at least some support and encouragement.

The reality, however, is these schools could not embody all of the defining attributes of an OBE system because they simply didn't control all of the factors needed to be a fully developed model. With a couple of contemporary exceptions that we will describe in Chapter 5, the schools usually lacked a clear framework of culminating outcomes of significance to use as the starting point for curriculum, instruction, and assessment and credentialing systems. Also missing in many cases was an authentically outcome-based assessment and reporting system. This was especially evident at the high school level, where testing, grading, and awarding of credits went on with few changes because they were defined and controlled through two powerful external forces: state graduation requirements and college admissions offices.

The reality. Unless districts and states are willing to grant individual schools waivers from some traditional regulations in order to get them to develop nontraditional prototypes — as in California, New York, and Texas — the best individual schools can hope to do is integrate OBE's purposes and principles into a best-possible configuration of Face 1, Face 2, and Face 4 features. As we will see in Chapter 5, some of these school-level models are quite stimulating, producing exciting learning results for students and inviting emulation by others.

13. By the criteria established here, is it possible for only part of a school or district to be outcome based?

The answer is similar to the previous one. The smaller the units of a total system that try to be outcome-based on their own, the more likely they will be compelled to conform to various traditional features of the larger system and to compromise the power of a totally integrated model. While it is not impossible for a portion of a school district to be outcome-based, without explicit support and endorsement from the highest levels of the system, the institutional inertia of the larger system will eventually wear these exceptional efforts down. When asked around 1980 to identify the key factor that led to successful implementation of Mastery Learning, proponents answered: "A strong and committed superintendent" — implying, of course, the existence of a board of education and community willing to let "success for all" happen in their schools.

A long way to go

For many years, individual teachers, teams of teachers, whole departments, and even whole schools have tried their best to apply the purposes and principles of OBE in their particular situations. The accumulated body of their individual successes kept the Face 1 and Face 2 approaches alive for 20 years. But outcome-based system change of the type suggested in the system transformation approach still lies on the horizon for most states and districts.

14. Are there recognized standards for OBE implementation?

Yes. In 1989, the High Success Program on OBE — now known as the High Success Network — was working with several consortia of school districts across the United States under the sponsorship of a small grant from the Danforth Foundation. As part of that effort, a set of operational standards consistent with OBE's purposes and principles was developed to guide district implementation efforts. Widely recognized as a basic foundation for successful implementation, that set of standards was modified slightly by the Network for Outcome-Based Schools in 1991 and by High Success the following year.

The standards address each of the components used in this chapter to describe the basic features of the four major configurations of OBE implementation and to connect closely the structural components of an OBE system (Figure 1.8 in Chapter 1) with OBE's four principles. The latest version of the standards listed below is the most comprehensive and comes closest to defining the components necessary for realizing the system transformation model.

Standards for OBE Implementation

1) A collectively endorsed mission statement that reflects staff commitment to:

   A. Achieving learning success for all students on future-focused, higher order exit outcomes essential to their future success as students and adults; and

   B. Implementing conditions and strategies that maximize all students' opportunities for success on these significant outcomes.

2) Clearly defined, publicly derived exit outcomes that:

   A. Directly reflect the knowledge, competencies, and performance orientations needed by positive contributing adults in an increasingly complex, changing world; and

   B. All students successfully demonstrate before they leave school.

3) A tightly articulated curriculum framework of outcome performances that:

   A. Is derived directly from these future-focused, higher order exit outcomes;

   B. Integrates knowledge, competence, and orientations across domains of learning; and

   C. Directly facilitates these exit outcomes.

4) A system of instructional decision making and delivery that consistently:

   A. Assures successful demonstration of all outcomes and performances for all students;

   B. Makes needed instruction available to students on a timely basis throughout the calendar year;

C. Employs a rich diversity of methods and strategies that encourages all students to be successful; and

D. Deliberately provides more than one uniform, routine chance for students to be successful, even after regular reporting periods and semesters have ended.

5) A criterion-based, consistently applied system of assessments, performance standards, student credentialing, and reporting that:

A. Is tightly aligned with all significant, future-focused exit outcomes;

B. Emphasizes applied learning in relevant, life-role contexts;

C. Encourages students to attain high performance levels on everything they pursue;

D. Documents what students do successfully whenever they are able to do it;

E. Enables students to demonstrate and receive full credit for improved learning on a timely basis anytime prior to graduation; and

F. Prevents and avoids invidious comparisons among students.

6) A system of instructional placement, grouping, and eligibility that enables students to advance through the curriculum whenever they can successfully demonstrate essential performance prerequisites for new learning experiences.

7) An ongoing system of program improvement that expands:

A. Staff vision of potential goals and modes of operation;

B. Staff accountability for the results of their decisions and practices;

C. Staff capacities for effective leadership, performance, renewal, and change; and

D. Structures that both encourage staff collaboration as well as support effective and responsive program implementation.

8) A database of significant, future-focused outcomes for all students plus other key indicators of school effectiveness, which is used and updated regularly to improve the conditions and practices that affect student and staff success.

15. Are there planning guides districts can use that are consistent with these implementation standards?

Yes. Two specifically were designed to be consistent with these standards, although both go beyond them in several important respects. One is the outcome-based action planning process developed by Charles Schwahn, which was mentioned near the end of Chapter 3. It focuses on 20 key dimensions critical to a thorough and successful implementation of either a program alignment or system transformation approach to OBE. Each of the 20 dimensions is a key component in one of four broad bases underlying any comprehensive change process. The four bases of successful change and their respective components (numbered consecutively) in Schwahn's planning framework are:

- PURPOSE: The fundamental reason for change to occur.

  1. Mission 2. Exit Outcomes 3. Organizational Vision

- OWNERSHIP: The personal and organizational commitment to change.

  4. Involvement of staff 5. Community/staff commitment

  6. Political support 7. Labor Relations

  8. Culture/Values/Beliefs

- CAPACITY: The technical ability of the organization's staff to change.

  9. Staff Selection 10. Staff Development

  11. Staff Empowerment 12. Staff Collegiality

  13. Instructional Technology

- SUPPORT: The structural opportunities for change to occur.

  14. Curriculum Development 15. Student Assessment

  16. Instructional Delivery 17. Risk Taking

  18. Policies and Procedures 19. Information Technology

  20. Budget

The other planning framework is a somewhat simpler diagnostic instrument for designing outcome-based restructuring developed by Alan Rowe of the College Community School District in Cedar Rapids, Iowa (see Chapter 5 for a more detailed description of OBE implementation in his district). Rowe's document enables district leaders to develop an extensive "Organizational Profile" of where their district and schools stand in relation to elements in 10 key components of an outcome-based system, including 1) outcomes; 2) measurement, evaluation, and assessment; 3) curriculum content and structure; 4) credentialing; 5) placement and advancement; 6) instructional delivery; 7) instructional patterns; 8) instructional methods; 9) personnel development; and 10) organizational development. All 10 of these components directly link with elements in the OBE implementation standards just described.

Summary

What are the most important things to remember about the major trends in OBE implementation? Before moving on to address the impact that OBE has on schools and learning, it is important to remember these six key things about OBE implementation trends:

1) Not all OBE is created equal.

2) Most of the early attempts to implement OBE thinking and principles in schools used micro-versions of outcomes, curriculum, time, and opportunity because they were natural extensions of traditional schooling practices.

3) The OBE movement has evolved dramatically during the past decade with theory outstripping the capacity of the field to find ways to implement the most macro-oriented, future-focused models.

4) Most state external accountability approaches to OBE vary enormously and do not embody its key principles, but they have drawn more attention to OBE in the past two years than all of the local initiatives have in the past 20 years.

5) There is a set of widely acknowledged standards for implementing OBE at the district and building levels that serves as the basis for comprehensive planning and implementation guides, which districts can use to assess their implementation readiness.

6) Partial implementation is far better than no implementation, but without encouragement and support from the top implementation often remains partial. Enormous traditional institutional inertia remains in place to counteract complete implementation.

Chapter 5
How Does Outcome-Based Implementation Affect Schools and Students?

T he purposes and principles of OBE explained in Chapter 1, the frameworks and examples of outcomes developed in Chapter 3, and the related configurations of OBE implementation shown in Chapter 4 lead us to two rather predictable answers to the major question of this chapter. First, OBE affects schools and students quite positively. Second, the effect depends on the approach the district or school in question has taken.

To answer this major question more precisely involves examining a variety of existing OBE models, simply because each has taken a different approach to defining its key outcomes, applying the four principles, and involving its community and staff in the implementation process. Consequently, this chapter will describe the highlights of OBE implementation as it is evolving at the district, building, and classroom levels. Some of the examples will involve districts that have been "at it" for more than 20 years; others will be schools that have been involved in OBE for less than two years but that have experienced something from which we can learn.

1. Is any one of these examples an "ideal" that others should emulate?

Few, if any, districts or schools have made all the paradigm changes described in the middle section of Chapter 2, but many are making every effort to do so.

However, many are undertaking the implementation process in the most comprehensive and prudent way possible, given the political, cultural, and economic realities of their community. In these cases, comprehensive implementation will take several years to achieve. Other schools and districts should use these examples as guides rather than as rigid models for their own efforts.

2. Why does comprehensive implementation take so long?

This answer has many parts, but we will focus on two of the most important. First, OBE represents a major change in how a long-established institution is defined, structured, and operated. It is not a package, program, or technique that can easily be installed inside the time-based system. OBE represents a fundamental transformation in the purposes, principles, and character of that system. Fundamental, deep-seated change does not come easily to any institution.

Second, districts involved with OBE for several years have discovered that the change, renewal, and improvement processes surrounding OBE are not "events" but ongoing ways of doing everything they do. As the concept of OBE has evolved dramatically over the past decade, so have districts' understandings of what "comprehensive implementation" means and what they must continuously attend to in order to realize the concept's potential. As we suggested in Chapter 4, those who initiated OBE in the '90s have frameworks, strategies, and templates to work with that simply didn't exist in the '80s. Each of these continues to evolve as implementers discover yet other ways to make OBE work more effectively for more students. And with every step a district wants to take up the Demonstration Mountain described in Chapter 3, the more the term "comprehensive implementation" is bound to depart from the familiar time-honored patterns of established practice.

3. What are some of the districts currently serving as models for others?

Three stand out as having a major national influence from the '80s to today: Johnson City, New York, Central Schools; Glendale, Arizona,

Union High School District; and Township High School District 214 in Arlington Heights, Illinois. Each has had exceptional district leadership and community support, and each has helped pioneer the evolution of OBE thinking and implementation on today's frontiers.

In addition, several other districts emerged as important early examples during the '90s. The most widely recognized U.S. districts include the Aurora, Colorado, Public Schools; College Community School District in Cedar Rapids, Iowa; Lucia Mar Unified School District in Arroyo Grande, California; Mooresville, North Carolina, Graded School District; and Yarmouth, Maine, School Department. Two key Canadian examples are the Waterloo County Board in Kitchener, Ontario, and the Yellowhead School Division in Edson, Alberta. While the list of districts "doing significant things" is much longer, most of them have not had the same degree of visibility or experience as those just noted.

4. How has OBE affected the schools and students in these districts?

Johnson City, New York, Central Schools

Nationally, the Johnson City Central Schools stand alone among OBE districts. A one-high-school-district in a moderately lower socioeconomic community, Johnson City began its OBE efforts in the early '70s under the leadership of then Superintendent John Champlin. The key forces driving their early work included the theory and research of John Carroll and Benjamin Bloom cited earlier, coupled with the district leadership's sense that Carroll and Bloom's thinking required comprehensive, total-system commitment and change to be implemented successfully. The core of the Johnson City model in those early days was a combination of individual-teacher and teacher-teaming approaches to Mastery Learning.

By the early '80s, Johnson City had established a strong record of student achievement gains in all the basic skills areas on both nationally normed standardized tests and on state-administered testing. By this time, they also had begun to see their high school students make major gains on the New York State Regents Examinations, which are used to determine eligibility for university admissions and scholarships. Most remarkable was the district's climb from last to first place on student performance among the 14 districts in its county on these standardized achievement measures.

With an initial decade of successful Mastery Learning implementation as background, Johnson City began to explore more deeply the research underlying staff empowerment and effectiveness, successful organizational change, and more powerful forms of student learning. They developed a framework of five key "learner outcomes" as a backdrop to all their academic instruction (positive self-concept, higher level cognitive skills, self-directed learner, social process skills, and concern for others); involved large numbers of staff in William Glasser's "Reality Therapy" approach to classroom management; and built an impressive culture of "success for all" among students and staff. This commitment to creating a context for successful learning for and by all students is one of the hallmarks of the Johnson City OBE approach, and it is reflected in the district's exceptional, success-oriented organizational climate.

The other hallmark is the district's approach to OBE implementation, the Outcome-Driven Developmental Model, known widely as ODDM. This approach is comprehensive, takes the total organization into account, and embodies a continuous improvement process grounded on asking and reconciling the answers to four key questions that serve as a decision screen for appropriate action. These include:

- What do you believe?
- What do you know?
- What do you want?
- What do you do?

These four questions compel staff to constantly match their beliefs and assumptions with the best knowledge in the field, with their goals for students, and with the realities of their daily practices and actions. Any mismatch is grounds for reconciling that element with "best knowledge."

(A more complete picture of the Johnson City approach and record is presented in an article by Ronald Brandt in the March 1994 issue of *Educational Leadership*, in which he interviewed Albert Mamary, Johnson City's Superintendent between 1982 and 1992.)

Glendale, Arizona, Union High School District

Glendale Union is a classic example of a district where OBE understanding and implementation continues to expand and mature over time. This nine-high-school, racially mixed district on Phoenix's northwest border began its OBE efforts in the late '70s when it established a comprehensive, rigorously designed, criterion-referenced testing system for all core academic subjects. This accountability-oriented testing system was administered to all 11,000 students each year. During the mid-1980s, under the leadership of Superintendent Gerald George and Assistant Superintendent Timothy Waters, the district began to explore how it might develop an instructional system that would strengthen student learning and be linked directly to this tightly designed testing system.

Five teachers, each from a different subject area, carried out the bulk of Glendale Union's instructional development work. The team started with a fairly conventional approach to Mastery Learning, but it rapidly evolved into a process they called Outcome-Based Instruction (OBI). The team's key breakthrough involved focusing the design of courses on the outcomes teachers wanted ALL their students to be able to demonstrate successfully at the end, rather than on a unit at a time. In the fully developed OBI model, lessons and units are treated as the means for getting to the course outcomes, not as culminating outcomes in themselves. The OBI strategy expanded the practical meaning and application of all four OBE principles (clarity of focus, expanded opportunity, high expectations, and design down), and it helped teachers realize that the true outcome of their courses didn't occur until June.

In addition, the five team members were given release time to plan together for districtwide implementation and to offer technical assistance to other teachers in the district's nine high schools as they sought it. After three years of initial implementation and the continuous spread of OBI into more and more classrooms, the district undertook the first formal evaluation of OBI's impact on student learning, using their existing criterion-referenced testing program as the appropriate assessment vehicle. The results were stunning:

- Regardless of subject area or family background characteristics (a universally powerful predictor of student achievement), students in OBI classes significantly outperformed their counterparts in conventional classrooms.

- The higher the degree of OBI implementation going on in a class, the higher the achievement advantages of those students, with students in "high implementation" classes scoring markedly higher than all others.

- Students with lower socioeconomic backgrounds who were in high implementation OBI classes actually outscored high socioeconomic students in conventional classrooms — an extremely rare finding under any instructional conditions.

During the '90s, Glendale Union expanded its horizons regarding "authentic" measures of student performance and turned its primary attention away from these multiple-choice measures. One of the new emphases is on student writing — a key component of their "Communicate Effectively" exit outcome. The strengths of their outcome-based efforts are evident on Arizona's 1993 Student Assessment Program for twelfth-graders. Among 21 districts of similar size, Glendale Union's students ranked first in the state in reading, second in math, and tied for first in writing — even though several of the comparison districts clearly ranked higher in terms of the socioeconomic backgrounds of their students. On the composite of these three measures, Glendale ranked first.

When they compared the quality of student writing on districtwide measures over time (with student socioeconomic backgrounds taken into account), Glendale Union discovered that 1) the overall quality of student writing improved steadily between 1989 and 1992, especially among students with lower socioeconomic backgrounds; and 2) their "Equity Index," reflecting the influence of family background on achievement, had declined over the same period, suggesting that student performance is increasingly less related to family circumstances than before. Both of these findings are significant pluses in terms of the purposes, premises, and principles of OBE, and they stand as a testimony to Glendale's continuing desire to use OBE as a vehicle for improving the learning of all students.

Township High School District 214, Arlington Heights, Illinois

As in the case of Johnson City and Glendale Union, District 214 has been a genuine trailblazer within the OBE movement during the past decade. Thanks to the insightful leadership of Associate Superintendent Kathleen Fitzpatrick, this predominantly middle class, six-high-school-district in Chicago's northwest suburbs was the first to:

- Develop a set of exit outcomes (called General Learner Outcomes — GLOs) that represent competencies critical to success beyond school for all students.

- Use their exit outcomes to develop the outcomes for their 10 key program areas.

- Devise and implement strategies for explicitly addressing those exit and program outcomes in all courses.

- Formalize criterion-based assessments at the classroom level for their exit outcomes.

- Require students to demonstrate all key outcomes in multiple contexts as a condition for graduation, effective with the class of 1995.

- Develop performance portfolios of significant outcome accomplishments as a supplement to traditional course and grade transcripts.

- Celebrate high-level achievement for all students who meet a defined performance standard by instituting a "Highest Honors Graduates" program in each school, in lieu of just a single valedictorian.

- Establish school accreditation standards through the North Central Association's "Outcomes Accreditation" process that are wholly consistent with the principles and components of an OBE system.

As a consequence of implementing these and other OBE components and processes over a decade, and despite a 20 percent decline in student enrollments over five years, District 214 has seen significant gains in:

- The number and percentage of students enrolled in advanced placement courses

- The number and percentage of students taking and passing advanced placement examinations

- The number of National Merit Finalists

- Districtwide scores on ACT and SAT examinations.

One key to the district's high-level achievements was that it developed and implemented a seven-step planning process:

1) Defining desired learning outcomes

2) Identifying criteria/indicators of the outcomes

3) Determining the context for outcome demonstrations

4) Designing high quality assessment tasks

5) Specifying performance standards

6) Developing a management plan for assessing outcomes of significance

7) Establishing support conditions for the development and implementation of a high quality curriculum and instructional system aligned with outcomes of significance.

Among those significant support conditions was District 214's constant attention to establishing strong community support and involvement in every component of this process. That support has been critical to their having moved forward as national leaders in many different implementation arenas.

Aurora, Colorado, Public Schools
Although its involvement with OBE did not begin until 1990, Aurora Public Schools has already established a national reputation as an innovator in outcome-based implementation. In January 1991, Aurora developed the first-ever exit outcome framework, which defined students as role performers rather than listing the knowledge or competencies they should develop. Districts throughout North America quickly adopted this

approach to defining exit outcomes. With some modification, it has emerged as the general standard in the field (see Chapter 3 for examples).

The impetus for developing a future-focused learner outcome framework came from two sources. One was a districtwide strategic planning effort started in 1989, which involved many members of Aurora's racially and socioeconomically diverse community. The other was the encouragement of two key curriculum specialists, Jane Pollack and Nora Redding.

In the fall of 1990, the district's communitywide Strategic Planning Committee joined forces with a districtwide design team under the leadership of current Superintendent David Hartenbach. Together they developed these five learner outcomes, based on an analysis of future trends, and a resulting set of 28 goals related to them:

SELF-DIRECTED LEARNER, who:

- Sets priorities and achievable goals

- Evaluates and manages own progress toward goals

- Creates options for self

- Takes responsibility for actions

- Creates a positive vision for self and future.

COLLABORATIVE WORKER, who:

- Evaluates and manages own behavior as a group member

- Evaluates and manages group functioning to meet the group's goal

- Demonstrates interactive communication

- Demonstrates consideration for individual differences.

COMPLEX THINKER, who:

- Effectively assesses, evaluates, and integrates information from a variety of resources

- Selects thinking processes appropriate to the resolution of complex issues

- Uses a wide variety of thinking processes with accuracy to resolve complex issues.

COMMUNITY CONTRIBUTOR, who:

- Demonstrates knowledge about his or her diverse communities
- Plans and takes action for the welfare of the community
- Reflects on role as a community contributor.

QUALITY PRODUCER, who:

- Creates products that achieve their purpose
- Creates products appropriate to the intended audience
- Creates products that reflect craftsmanship
- Uses resources/technology.

These five learner outcomes pervade everything done at Aurora. They provide a universal focus and purpose for all instruction and are used to design curriculum, organize and deliver instruction, assess student performance, and develop portfolios of significant student learning. Rubrics — or frameworks of critical performance criteria — have been developed for each of the five learner outcomes and all courses of study include them.

However, based on input from parents, staff, and community, Aurora translated this learner outcome orientation into a performance-based program that stresses subject-area content, while requiring students to demonstrate clearly what they have learned. Known as Performance-Based Education (PBE), this effort defines basic content as well as role performances. The Aurora community needed to see solid content as an end, not just as a means to an end.

Consequently, Aurora also has developed a framework of K-12 content outcomes for nine major program areas. The knowledge and skills students learn through the content allows them to be role performers as defined in the learner outcomes. These content outcomes, or proficiencies, provide students with the enabling knowledge and skills needed to perform successfully and meet the district's mission of developing lifelong learners.

Implementation is tailored to each of Aurora's 42 schools according to a shared decision-making arrangement between the district and each school. Meanwhile, the nerve center of this process is the district's three-pronged assessment model. The model comprehensively assesses content outcomes and the five learner outcomes.

The benefits of portfolios. One assessment component is the portfolio. It is designed to provide tangible evidence of the student's knowledge, abilities, and growth in becoming a self-directed, lifelong learner. The portfolio is student-centered, allows considerable student choice in its composition, may involve obtaining input from mentors and other advisers, includes a student self-evaluation based on agreed-on rubrics and criteria, and involves the student presenting its content to an audience — often at parent conferences.

The second component, secured assessments, matches the content proficiencies in the curriculum, which also are used to assess the complex thinker and quality producer learner outcomes. Secured assessments typically are administered under controlled time and performance conditions in which the student is aware of the general knowledge and skills being assessed, but must perform specific tasks without help or without knowing the exact content ahead of time. These assessments are scored by trained graders thoroughly familiar with the content and standards in question.

The third component is called validations, which are opportunities to carry out what are often called "authentic" assessments. Multiple sources of information are applied against a universal set of district-established criteria for either content or learner outcomes. Often validations include a combination of direct observation, student self-reporting, authentic classroom tasks, and traditional tests. They often occur with students carrying out the same demonstration processes but with different content and in diverse settings. Two of their key purposes are to assess important student behaviors, such as self-directedness or collaborative skills, and to encourage both students and staff to regard learning as more comprehensive than mental activity alone.

Overall, the Aurora assessment program has four key purposes: 1) instructional — to guide what gets taught and learned; 2) documentation of the content and learner outcomes — to produce direct evidence about all of the criteria that constitute the content and learner outcomes; 3) self-reflection — to have students assess their own progress against established criteria; and 4) showcasing — to allow and encourage students to display exemplary "artifacts" of their achievement in a multidimensional, long-term, authentic fashion.

Instructional evidence can include works showing learning and growth, student purposes, resumes and autobiographies, and visual or audio records of improved performances. Documentation of the content and learner outcomes can include evidence pertaining to authentic tasks, references from others, extracurricular accomplishments, lab reports, recorded performances, and published works. Self-reflection can include journal entries, autobiographies or self-portraits, and post-it notes with brief evaluations on them. Showcasing can include authentic assessments, resumes, inventions or experiments, performances or displays, published work, awards, and job information. Documentation, self-reflection, and showcasing are all intended to have multiple audiences: students, parents, teachers, peers, and community members.

The culminating manifestation of all this performance evidence is Aurora's "Proposed Graduation Requirements for the Class of 1999." In June 1992, a task force of over 50 students, teachers, administrators, parents, board members, community members, and state policymakers proposed that beginning with the class of 1999, graduation from the Aurora Public Schools be contingent on the successful demonstration all of the district's content and learner outcomes. Evidence from all three assessment modes is required. All assessing and grading would be done "in pencil" to allow students continual opportunities to improve their record and portfolio. District diplomas and transcripts would document the level of accomplishment on each content and learner outcome. These requirements would put into policy and practice what many OBE districts have assumed is the ultimate embodiment of exit outcome standards.

According to teachers and district staff, the biggest effects of the district's PBE efforts on students so far are 1) students having a very clear purpose and sense of direction instructionally, 2) a strong feeling that "clarity of focus" and criteria by teachers have eliminated "game-playing" in the classroom, 3) constant, active learning by students in classrooms, 4) a strong sense of students taking responsibility for their own learning success, and 5) a high sense of pride in what they accomplish.

College Community School District, Cedar Rapids, Iowa

As in every district mentioned so far, OBE's initiation and success in the College Community School District has been due to exceptional efforts of one or more local champions. In this case, Assistant Superintendent Alan Rowe, who doubles as the codirector of the Iowa Success Network, together with a consortium of over 25 Iowa school districts and major universities, supports cutting-edge OBE implementation in the state.

College Community has focused its OBE implementation process around its mission: to ensure quality learning today for tomorrow.

Fusing the premises, principles, and practices of OBE with the late W. Edwards Deming's Theory of Profound Knowledge and quality management tools, the district has immersed itself in a continuous learning and improvement mindset. This orientation emanates from its exit outcomes, which are viewed as continuous improvement life roles: self-directed learners, responsible citizens, complex thinkers, and effective communicators.

Uniquely, College Community has based its efforts around the notion that exit outcomes 1) are to be modeled by all adults in the organization, 2) must be modeled by the organization itself (through its policies, procedures, practices, and priorities), and 3) most of all, must be demonstrated by all students through authentic performance tasks with clearly established quality criteria.

Specifically, the district diligently seeks operational consistency and alignment in the following ways: student performance, adult performance, and organizational performance. The key student performance elements include:

- Student-led parent conferences

- Authentic life role performance tasks

- Student use of total quality management tools

- Performance benchmarks in reading, writing, and applied mathematical thinking in grades 4, 8, and 10

- A technical literacy course requirement

- Performance requirements for high school entry

- Integrated, multimedia performances

- A specialized mini-course program.

The key adult performance elements include:

- Faculty performance portfolios
- Principal performance portfolios
- Staff development in demonstration task design, rubrics and assessment criteria, new national standards, and total quality management tools
- Peer coaching model
- Quality customer service design system.

The key organizational performance elements include:

- Performance-based curriculum design framework
- Performance diploma requirements
- Statistical process control charting for system accountability
- Block schedule at the high school
- Multiage classrooms
- Multiyear contracts for staff
- Schoolwide enrichment models
- District quality council (for building an intense customer focus).

These alignment elements and approaches continue to foster and enrich a spirit of stakeholder support for College Community's continuous improvement journey, and they make it a pioneer among OBE districts pursuing the system transformation model described in Chapter 4.

Lucia Mar Unified School District, Arroyo Grande, California

Unlike Aurora and College Community, who initiated their OBE efforts in the '90s when the notion of future-driven exit outcomes was fairly well established, the Lucia Mar Unified School District began its school improvement efforts in 1987 by focusing on improving instruction in the basic curriculum: reading, mathematics, science, and social studies.

Joseph Boeckx, who was then the district's new superintendent, became a highly visible champion of OBE efforts. He recognized the district's 15 schools, its instructional programs, and its expectations for students were focused almost entirely on meeting the needs of local agricultural and tourist-based service economies. Over 30 percent of Lucia Mar's 10,000 students were from non-English speaking families, and community expectations for educating them beyond high school were limited. In 1987, the California State Department of Education classified Lucia Mar as a low-performing district, but Boeckx and his board of education knew it could improve.

What began as a classic example of a program alignment approach to instructional improvement evolved into a strong system transformation approach to OBE as a result of Boeckx's insistence that the district operate according to six key principles:

1) That all decisions be based on sound research rather than on convention or convenience.

2) That the entire K-12 curriculum be carefully aligned around clearly defined outcomes in four major subject areas: reading, math, science, and social studies.

3) That teaching the aligned curriculum is every teacher's responsibility.

4) That the district develop and implement a criterion-based assessment system built around and tightly aligned with its curriculum outcomes (thereby eliminating standardized tests as indicators of instructional success).

5) That staff evaluation be based on the successful teaching of the aligned curriculum.

6) That a climate of stability and trust within the district be established, based on collaborative decision making, high accessibility of the superintendent to all staff and the community, and the establishment of a win-win bargaining approach with staff.

The continuous focus on and implementation of the first principle, plus its direct impact on the other five, eventually led Lucia Mar from thoroughly examining the best available school reform and restructuring initiatives of the '80s (its program alignment orientation to OBE) to a major focus in the '90s on implementing and assessing exit and program outcomes. These program outcomes match the high-tech labor market of today and tomorrow. In effect, this evolution shifted the instructional focus from discrete content skill outcomes to a much more expansive emphasis on authentic problem solving.

Today, this new orientation is manifested in the district's Systems and Discovery Center. Eleven major corporations and three colleges are actively collaborating with Lucia Mar to 1) define new performance standards for Lucia Mar's students that match world-market criteria and 2) build new performance models that involve students applying these competencies in on-the-job settings.

This intensive, seven-year commitment to making the district's six principles work and to making the purposes and principles of OBE come alive in its schools has resulted in major academic gains for students. Over the last four years, the district's elementary school students' scores have risen steadily on California's mandated testing programs in all curriculum areas. Lucia Mar is now performing higher than most California districts with similar socioeconomic characteristics, and as well as many districts with much higher socioeconomic communities. Over the same period, dramatic improvements have occurred at the high school level in four major areas:

1) Student dropout rates have plummeted.

2) The percentage of students taking advanced placement courses has risen dramatically.

3) The percentage of students taking and passing advanced placement exams for college credit has risen as sharply.

4) The percentage of students applying to and attending a community college or university has doubled.

All of these changes occurred in the face of major budget cuts, the release of more than 100 district staff, and increases in average class size from 27 to 31 students.

Mooresville, North Carolina, Graded School District

Although "the newest kid on the block" among districts with an emerging national reputation in OBE, Mooresville stands out as an example of establishing all of the conditions and pieces that make a comprehensive system transformation approach to OBE possible. Led by local champion Pam Beaver, Mooresville spent over a year studying major school reform and restructuring approaches and the factors needed to make them successful before formalizing any implementation planning. The district's thorough and cautious approach to laying a solid groundwork for successful change has worked well for them in their strongly traditional community and has drawn sincere praise from districts in similar circumstances.

The crucial year of study, planning, grant writing, and initial implementation in Mooresville was 1992. Key staff attended several OBE conferences and seminars and prepared a grant proposal to become a North Carolina OBE pilot site. Their proposal declared Mooresville's commitment to a ". . . shift from time-based, curriculum-driven education to an outcome-based, future-driven school system" that fully embraced a system transformation approach to OBE. The district received the state grant in August 1992, then launched a full-scale implementation effort.

As in Iowa's College Community School District, the Mooresville approach to OBE is a synthesis of cutting-edge work on quality systems and the High Success Network's future-focused, transformational model of OBE. Their vision is to be a total quality system, and accomplishing this means developing and integrating nine critical components of organizational functioning and change:

1) A future-driven orientation to program building

2) Outcomes of significance for all learners

3) Enlightened, visionary leadership throughout the district

4) A community-of-learners professional culture

5) Shared decision making with all key stakeholders

6) A success-for-all philosophy toward learners and staff

7) A relevant, outcome-driven curriculum

8) Expanded opportunities for learners to succeed

9) Technology and community partnerships.

Developing and implementing all nine of these components is a formidable, continuous task. But several things stand out as guides to others.

First, Mooresville spent a great deal of time establishing a clear direction for its improvement efforts. The results of this extensive process are reflected in its decisive vision statement, its district beliefs, its districtwide mission statement, and its framework of future-focused exit outcomes, which fully develop the following role performance expectations for all graduates:

- Continuously developing, lifelong, self-directed LEARNER
- Responsible, concerned COMMUNICATOR
- Quality WORKER
- Prudent FINANCIAL PLANNER
- Involved CITIZEN
- Well-rounded PERSON

Second, the district excelled at communicating with and involving all key stakeholder groups in every phase of planning and direction setting. Intensive efforts were made to get staff and community involved in meetings and planning sessions. Public service announcements and a viewer-friendly videotape were developed and broadcast frequently on local stations. An original and now popular song, "Learning for Tomorrow, Today!" was sung at all school functions.

One tangible result of these intensive outreach efforts was getting more than 500 community members out to three different informational meetings and involving hundreds of them in the strategic design process that led to the development of exit outcomes.

Third, to allay parental concerns about the meaning and implications of the major changes taking place, the district established a formal set of "Assurances." These assurances were pledges to parents, staff, and the community that no extreme changes would be made without serious study over a significant period of time. Also, staff and the public would be involved in deciding when and if better practices should replace existing ones. The heart of the document is 18 specific statements that clearly state where various responsibilities lie, what will be emphasized, and how things will be done in the district. District leaders believe this document has been the key to gaining support for their change process.

Fourth, in keeping with the overall outcome-based thrust of their vision and mission, Mooresville decided to address explicitly the "Enlightened, Visionary Leadership" component of their effort by clearly defining the role of the instructional leader and deriving a set of performance outcomes for him or her. Charles Schwahn facilitated the process using a framework of key bases and spheres of change developed by the High Success Network. Six things emerged from the process:

1) Criteria and a quality performance demonstration framework for Instructional Leaders.

2) Commitment to operate the district's administrative team as a "Community of Learners."

3) Criteria and a quality performance demonstration framework for Visionary Leaders who can set a purpose for change.

4) Criteria and a quality performance demonstration framework for Consensus Builders who can develop staff and community ownership for successful change.

5) Criteria and a quality performance demonstration framework for Enabling Leaders who can develop organizational and staff capacity for successful change.

6) Criteria and a quality performance demonstration framework for Supportive Leaders who can establish support and organizational opportunities for successful change.

While implementation of this comprehensive effort has only been underway since 1993, it already has withstood political attacks from outside the district by groups opposed to OBE.

Yarmouth, Maine, School Department

Like Mooresville, Yarmouth has been involved in comprehensive OBE design since 1992. It has followed a similar path of engaging in a comprehensive strategic planning effort with Charles Schwahn, establishing a great deal of staff and community involvement and support, and setting a powerful purpose and direction for the entire instructional program. Under the leadership of Superintendent Kenneth Murphy, Yarmouth has committed itself to making an already successful 2,000-student district even "more excellent."

Districts hoping to learn about successful OBE implementation strategies from Yarmouth will find the following elements:

- A strong district focus manifested through a powerful mission statement defining why the district exists; a framework of 11 core values that underlie all district decisions and actions; a framework of future-focused, life-role exit outcomes linked to six critical arenas of living: economics, relationships, global, cultural and recreational, civic, and learning; clearly articulated beliefs regarding students and learning, school staff and teaching, and school and community; and an extensive vision statement that describes exactly what Yarmouth intends to be in the future.

- Clearly defined participatory teams for designing and implementing all the programmatic pieces needed to achieve the exit outcomes and implement all facets of the district strategic plan. These include school improvement teams of teachers and administrators at each site, a district improvement team of staff from each building plus the chair of the district's school committee, and districtwide content area groups enabling all teachers to link their curriculum directly to the district's exit outcomes and to determine curriculum content priorities.

- A district "blueprint" planning process that details the steps each school will take over the next three years to implement the focus of the strategic plan.

- An implementation framework that drives the ultimate realization of the strategic plan. The key components in this framework are 1) the school blueprints; 2) a K-12 assessment process; 3) a framework of K-12 "Essential Knowledge" outcomes; 4) the development of sample assessments for the essential knowledge outcomes; 5) the design of rubrics, process/product standards, and quality checks; 6) the design of pilot quality assessments; and 7) logistics and operational factors — all leading to the improvement of student learning through teamwork.

- A framework of outcomes for the district's seven major learning areas patterned on the exit outcome framework. These areas include math, language arts, science, social studies, foreign language, special services, and unified arts — the latter combining seven specialized curricular areas.

When integrated and applied over the next three years, these five major elements will help Yarmouth achieve its mission: to empower all students to create fulfilling lives in a changing world.

5. How has OBE affected schools and students in other districts?

While many districts come to mind, the experiences of three districts in southern Michigan are very similar and embody a typical profile of districts that began implementing OBE in the early '90s. The three districts are: Howell Public Schools, Walled Lake Consolidated Schools, and the Waterford School District. Howell is located about 70 miles west of Detroit, and Walled Lake and Waterford are in the outer ring of Detroit's suburbs.

All three districts were heavily involved in various OBE conferences and training seminars over a three-year period. Each is an active member of the Michigan-Ohio-Ontario Consortium on OBE, and each has developed a framework of role performance outcomes similar to those in Aurora, Mooresville, and Yarmouth. Finally, each district has an OBE local champion: Deputy Superintendent Alberta Ellis in Howell; Coordinator of Staff Development Sandra Feeley in Walled Lake; and Assistant Superintendent Larry Strong in Waterford. This common background of training experiences and complex exit outcomes is undoubtedly one of the reasons their experiences have been so similar. Consequently, the following pages will be a composite profile of the three districts, although each has its own particular configuration of practices, circumstances, and results.

Here's what the Michigan districts report about the impact of a framework of role performance outcomes on curriculum, staff roles, and students:

- The definition of student learning has changed dramatically. It now involves a wider scope as well as a greater depth than before. Content memorization has given way to in-depth exploration of issues and engagement in complex projects.

Teachers are teaching students what quality learning means, and students are applying those standards to themselves and to each other.

- Because students see a clear purpose and greater relevance to learning than before, student learning as measured by both standard testing programs and by the complexity and quality of their work is increasing steadily. Students across the board regularly do much more in-depth work than before.

- Curriculum design and instruction has a common focus and purpose that goes miles beyond what is in textbooks. District curriculum frameworks and the outcomes for programs, courses, and units are either derived from or judged against exit outcomes. The standards for using and teaching content have changed accordingly.

- Faculty interaction, planning, and teaming across subjects and grade levels has increased dramatically as teachers recognize their efforts are aligned toward a common goal. In addition, far more staff interaction is focused on the serious issues surrounding curriculum design, instructional processes, and/or student assessment.

- Integrated, thematic instruction structured around issues and problems relevant to students is now common. These units and major projects encourage in-depth exploration and involvement by students and have increased significantly the motivation and learning success of formerly at-risk students.

- The number of authentic assessment designs and practices has increased significantly as staff at all levels and in all areas create performance experiences for students patterned around the complexity of the exit outcomes. Paper and pencil tests and standard report cards are giving way to more active demonstrations of complex learning, performance portfolios, and student-led conferences for both parents and future teachers regarding their learning accomplishments.

- Because so much about these system transformation approaches to OBE is new and requires expanded contexts for student learning, a great deal of continuous contact with parents and other community members has occurred.

In addition, individual districts offer these particular observations:

- School staffs are now much more research-oriented as they seek better ways to do things.
- "Old system" definitions and rationales for things don't hold water any longer. Staff recognize that many old practices are obsolete and must be changed.
- All staff in the system see their roles differently than before. Expectations for quality performance are higher, and involvement is greater.
- Because instruction focuses more on in-depth concepts, students grasp the meaning of things faster and learn better.
- Students take responsibility for contributing to curriculum design, hold themselves more accountable than teachers do, and treat learning as their top priority in school.
- Staff professionalism has increased as more of them have received in-depth training and had opportunities to present their work at conferences and training sessions.

While this list does not exhaust the trends that emerged in these three districts, it gives some indication of the impact a clearly focused and committed OBE implementation effort can have on schools and students. It also illustrates and reinforces several things that hold true for every example described in this chapter:

- The culture and climate of the organization change.
- Innovation becomes imperative.
- Everyone is compelled to go into "learning mode."
- Both staff and students take on new definitions of their roles.
- Both success and "professionalism" increase.

- A common purpose surfaces.

- Both people and their organizations stretch beyond conventional boundaries.

6. How has OBE implementation affected staff and students in individual schools?

Without question, each of the examples provided in this chapter relates to what is occurring in school buildings and classrooms, not just their central offices. Nonetheless, some school-based examples of OBE deserve particular mention because of their stature within the field and the uniqueness of their implementation efforts. One of them is the Southridge Middle School in Fontana, California, a very heterogeneous community located about 60 miles east of Los Angeles. The other is Champlin Park High School in the Anoka-Hennepin School District, a large suburban district just north of Minneapolis.

Southridge Middle School

Southridge fits the image of what we might expect from an innovative, future-focused, outcome-based middle school in ethnically diverse southern California. Organized around its own compelling framework of exit outcomes, the school is structured around interdisciplinary teams; uses longer than normal scheduling blocks; has institutionalized a work-hard/play-hard culture; is a hotbed of focused, purposeful innovation; has successfully tapped the motivation and learning potential of its 1,300 students; has reached out to parents and the larger community in exceptional ways; holds several state and national awards for excellence; and, finally, has a staff of award-winning, professionally involved teachers.

The catalyst for this system transformation in action is Gary Soto, Southridge's national award-winning principal and the champion of its OBE efforts. Soto and the Southridge staff have developed a delicate balance among several critical factors that fuel continuous evolution of OBE design and implementation: high energy, patience, assurances of support for risk taking, technical rigor, high enthusiasm, common focus, autonomy, collaboration, adventure, celebration, and individual trailblazing. These elements are combined into an organizational mix that forms a deeply felt commitment to having every student emerge a capable, collaborative, self-directed learner and citizen.

The keys to making the technical side of Southridge's program work are:

- The development of performance criterion frameworks, consistent with each of their key outcomes, to guide staff planning and student learning.

- Team-based instructional planning and delivery.

- Major investments in staff planning time and support, which enable staff to develop challenging, interdisciplinary instructional units to motivate and deeply engage students.

- Continuous movement toward a criterion-based system of assessment, evaluation, record-keeping, and reporting for all students; with exit outcomes of significance and performance rubrics and portfolios as the foundation.

- A strong and focused staff development program, with a continuous review of emerging research trends, quality performances, and quality assessments as its core.

- A strong service learning focus for students.

- A powerful student-led conferencing model in which all 1,300 students carry out at least two reports to their parents each year, one at school and one at home.

Over the past three years, student attendance at Southridge has climbed to the 99 percent level, student achievement on both tests and teacher grades shows a steady and major improvement, and staff attitudes toward school reform have become significantly more positive. The school's biggest challenges: 1) continuing to expand and improve its criterion-based assessment system and 2) handling the nearly 1,000 visitors it receives each year.

Champlin Park High School

Champlin Park High is an OBE story in the making. This four-year high school of 2,200 students opened its doors in fall 1992, explicitly designed and built to facilitate a "house" structure, extensive use of computers, and advanced applications of OBE. Champlin Park's initial claim to fame, however, is its dramatically restructured delivery schedule designed to embody the "less is more" thinking of Essential Schools founder Theodore Sizer: much longer, in-depth class periods and fewer students for teachers.

In spring 1991, the school's principal and OBE champion, David Bonthuis, selected department leaders from a large pool of district staff who had transferred from Anoka-Hennepin's other high schools. They spent a year considering a variety of options and planning for the school's opening the next fall. Central to their discussions was how to organize the school's four houses of 550 students, how to define the OBE approach they were going to take, and how to schedule the day and the year to best support 1) consistent implementation of OBE's clarity of focus, expanded opportunity, high expectations, and design down principles; 2) availability of courses for students; 3) smaller class sizes; 4) flexible forms of instructional time; 5) improved instruction and student retention; and 6) teacher contract requirements. Their ultimate goals: a better learning environment and more opportunities for students, and a healthier, more productive, saner environment for teachers.

Based on a variety of programmatic and fiscal considerations, Champlin Park opened its doors operating on a schedule of three 95-minute periods per day. In 1993-94, the schedule shifted to four 85-minute periods per day, the staff's original preference. While no formal evaluation has been done on this significant restructuring effort, evidence of staff and student support abounds. This suggests that the Champlin Park model and its marriage of technology, a house system, OBE, and time restructuring — occurring in a state with an outcome performance graduation policy — is an example worth watching closely.

7. How has OBE implementation affected classroom practice and student learning?

Volumes could be written in response to this question, and each could feature a particular approach to OBE. Instead, we will focus on only four examples — chosen because they represent different fields, geographical areas, grade levels, and delivery configurations. But all four embody two critical elements: 1) a serious attempt to make role performance exit outcomes come alive in the classroom and 2) a deep commitment to the purposes, premises, and principles of OBE.

The Challenger Elementary School Team

The first example involves Diane Wright and Beth Dhue, two teachers at Challenger Elementary School in Howell, Michigan. They co-teach 60 fifth-graders in the same room. Their arrangement works because each has a distinctive style that complements the other. One is more skill-oriented and analytical; the other, more insightful and intuitive.

Together Wright and Dhue are working to develop their students' performances on Howell's eight exit outcomes to the highest levels, particularly as they can connect them to major life issues outside of school. Student outcomes include being self-directed learners, higher level thinkers, collaborative contributors, innovative producers, community participants, adaptable problem solvers, physically and emotionally able individuals, and knowledgeable people. One inherent component of their teaching is to design and employ quality criteria to guide all student performances on these outcomes; another is student collaboration.

The major breakthrough in their desire to link students' classroom learning closer to real-life experience came during the 1992-93 school year following the Hurricane Andrew disaster in Florida. Their local PTA group suggested that the students collect much-needed supplies for a seriously damaged elementary school. The students decided to turn the short-term endeavor into a longer commitment, so they 1) formed a nonprofit organization called Kids Who Kare (KWK), 2) wrote to the damaged school to determine their needs, 3) developed the focus of a fundraising project to buy supplies for the school (collecting pop cans), 4) kept careful records on their collections, 5) developed a collection incentive plan for their school, 6) handled all financial accounting, 7) wrote letters to local businesses enlisting their help, and 8) developed an extensive advertising campaign for local media to advertise their project. By June, they had raised $1,000, plus supplies and gift certificates donated by local businesses. A whole range of academic skills were eagerly honed and applied during this undertaking.

In 1993-94, the students' project focused on a local environmental problem and ended up receiving national attention. A former lubrication/paint/soap manufacturing company in the community had filed for bankruptcy and had left its site seriously polluted with toxic chemicals. In this case, the students, with supervision from their teachers:

- Heard a presentation by the Michigan Department of Natural Resources (MDNR) on the site.

- Drafted proclamations and wrote letters to community leaders and a variety of public officials and state legislators encouraging clean-up of the site.

- Received both positive letters and decisive action from a host of major public officials in response to their letters, including a letter of commendation from the MDNR.

- Met with U.S. Senator Levin regarding their mutual support of the site clean-up.

- Heard a presentation by the Environmental Protection Agency's site director on the state of present clean-up activities that resulted from their initiatives and received a plaque from the EPA acknowledging their work in protecting the environment.

- Received major coverage from the local press for their project.

- Developed a subsequent schoolwide recycling project.

- Initiated a communitywide advertising campaign to support the project and to urge respect for the environment.

- Undertook several fundraising projects to collect money for the EPA's Super Fund and became part of a national documentary video intended for its support.

- Received an invitation from the EPA to form a school-business partnership with them using computer technology as a means of communication.

- Received constant coaching and feedback from their teachers regarding the continuous attention they needed to give to the purpose, audiences, substance, quality, and assessment of their projects.

For Wright and Dhue, the key outcomes were neither the funds for the Florida school nor the clean-up of the toxic waste site, but what the students learned about constantly facing the issue: "How do we measure achievement?" What Wright and Dhue call "authentic assessment projects" give students a reason to learn and work hard, and they find this reason reflects itself in all students' other schoolwork. Given the impetus of these projects and design models provided by Wright and Dhue, these students have become inventors of their own curricula and now spontaneously and continually initiate and research topics of personal interest.

A Challenger Elementary "Teacher-As-Learner" Example

The second example relates to the experiences of one of their Challenger Elementary colleagues, a first-grade teacher named Lynn Henderson. The Henderson story has two clear parts: how she worked with a very challenging class of students, and what she learned about learning from that experience. Both illustrate much of the thinking and practice that underlie the system transformation approach to OBE, and what happens when teachers and students are guided by the kinds of exit outcomes that Howell has developed.

In fall 1993, Henderson inherited a class of students that previous teachers, substitutes, and a variety of specialists characterized as having behavioral problems. She saw them as bright, capable, challenging, and fractious, but she began the year with 1) a strong conviction that they all could learn, 2) an extensive repertory of instructional skills, 3) an orientation toward authentic learning activities, and 4) an expectation that they had to meet state basic skills standards. The latter issue and the students' behavior lurked in the background.

Through the use of active learning strategies, group research projects, authentic performance assessments, public performances, portfolios, and student-led conferencing, Henderson realized in March that virtually all of her students had already more than met the state's basic skills standards, and that the rest of the year could be spent using and expanding them to the fullest. The turning point in her year was the realization that, while others had continually focused on what the students couldn't do (behave quietly), she had managed to tap their enormous energy and motivation and had, instead, focused on what they could do, which was learn.

Henderson's formal self-assessment reveals a lot about what really happens when teachers' visions of their work change and new sets of possibilities arise. Her personal self-assessment of her year includes the following observations that quite explicitly reveal a lot about the impact of OBE on classrooms and students:

- "It is not the limitations of the children but their strengths that get the job done."

- "Structure is important at first, but once it's learned, it can be ignored."

- "It isn't finishing papers that shows what kids know."

- "You can move to real-life activities even when they don't all know how to sit still and listen."

- "Once the structure of completing work is taught, the process of observing, recording, and hypothesizing becomes the core curriculum."

- "I can be a 'guide on the side' even though I adore being the 'sage on the stage.'"

- "The very thing I have fought all year and struggled against, the thing which I saw as willfulness, is really independence, and I have finally come to appreciate it. In fact, it is the thing I most treasure in people. I didn't recognize it in children so young because I did not expect to see it. I am a little disappointed in that. . .I was teaching them as if they were mindless, when they knew what they needed better than I."

The Gananda OBE Senior Demonstration

The third example concerns the culminating demonstration of district role performance exit outcomes by graduating high school seniors supervised by a team of their teachers. This unique example of outcome-based implementation occurs at Gananda Central School in Walworth, New York, and was initiated for the class of 1993 by James Ludington, an OBE math teacher at the school.

What is called the OBE Senior Demonstration is a tightly structured project designed and carried out by the entire senior class as a supplement to their regular academic program. It is designed to:

- Demonstrate the district's three exit outcomes (effective communicator, accountable citizen, and self-directed learner) as a condition for graduation.

- Link school learning to the major spheres and arenas of living.

- Implement the principles of "Transformational OBE."

- Accomplish significant, clearly defined performances as a culmination of their high school careers.

- Contribute something of genuine value to the community.

- Emanate from the ideas and commitment of the students themselves.

Student orientation to and preparation for the project involves eight clearly identified components, including generating key issues; undertaking a consensus-building process using a team approach to resolving problems; establishing brainstorming committees and selecting students to participate in each, and defining committee and individual brainstorming responsibilities. In addition, the students must develop protocols for class meetings, establish ground rules for committee interactions, practice presentation skills for peer and outside evaluators (because committees will have to present their ideas and plans to community and governmental bodies), contact outside community resources for assistance and support, and define and alter committee functions and working timetables.

Beyond that, students are responsible for 1) identifying and carrying out 21 different skills and attributes essential to the success of the project, 2) identifying the key working committees that will be necessary to carry out the project and the functions each will have to perform, 3) staffing and implementing those working committees, 4) establishing and implementing a monitoring process that assures all of the key components of the project are proceeding successfully and on schedule, and 5) tracking their own involvement in the project and assessing what they are contributing and learning.

The 1992-93 project involved the design and construction of a sidewalk that would link two communities and allow young children to walk to school without having to be on a narrow, busy roadway. The project was accepted and the sidewalk built. The 1994 project involved developing a ballot referendum to generate taxes for the construction of an auditorium for the high school. At this writing, the ultimate fate of the auditorium construction project had not been determined.

Despite the major responsibility placed on students to define and carry out the project, the five faculty advisors (Ludington, Sandi Hamilton,

Dennis Greco, Cynthia Carroll, and Mark Pellegrino) play an invaluable role in facilitating, providing direction, scheduling, teaching, evaluating, and monitoring each component and phase of the project. This endeavor is a dramatic example of making the system transformation approach to OBE real at the high school level.

The Boone Education Loop Reading Project

The fourth example links the beginning and end of students' public school careers together in one integrated endeavor. The Education Loop Reading Project is the outgrowth of what began as a collaborative effort between Barbara Benson, a senior English teacher at Watauga High School in Boone, North Carolina, and one of her first-grade teacher colleagues, Susy Barnett. While both regularly use most of the system transformation approaches to OBE with great success in their individual classes, they discovered a way of helping high school seniors address and accomplish their high school's goals and North Carolina's draft set of exit outcomes (confident and competent individuals, self-directed learners, complex thinkers, supportive persons, contributing citizens, cooperative team members, and quality producers), while performing a valuable educational and community service at the same time.

Reading partners. The heart of the Ed Loop Project is a direct personal link between each high school senior and one or more first-grade students who become their "reading partners." The seniors prepare rigorously in their English class for their once-a-month visits to the elementary school to read to their partners. The seniors must get library cards, select appropriate books for their partners to use, make tapes of the books to leave with their partners, prepare a lesson plan for carrying out the Ed Loop visit, write a self-assessment of each visit using performance criteria, problem solve after each visit to improve their performance on the next visit, and make books as gifts for their partners.

The younger students, in return, write a reaction to each visit, write letters to their reading partners, prepare some of their own work to share during the visit, listen to the tapes as they re-read the books their seniors left for them that month, answer the comprehension questions on their book tapes, practice being good listeners, and learn from a responsible, supportive high school student.

The impact of the project, based on teacher observations, insightful student self-reports, and touching parent letters, has been extremely positive. For the seniors, it has promoted an understanding of good children's literature and the importance of reading to their own children when they become parents. In addition, it has involved them in the important community task of helping others learn to read, sharpened their awareness of child development and the challenges of parenting, taught them critical focusing and organizational skills, increased their sense of personal and community responsibility, placed them in the role of competent and responsible mentors and role models, improved their attendance and performance in school, taught them the importance of designing and accomplishing high quality tasks, and, of course, greatly improved their English skills and performance.

The personal bonds established during the two years of Ed Loop's existence and the role modeling it provides have resulted in all of the younger students, with their parents, attending the high school graduation of their reading partner. And by all accounts, the most orderly and responsible behavior on the part of seniors at graduation in memory!

Summary

What are the most important things to remember about how OBE affects schools and students? The examples shared in this chapter reveal a rich array of approaches to the implementation of OBE and a variety of very positive results for staff and students. Among them, five things stand out:

1) Successful implementation at both the district and building levels is inseparable from community understanding and involvement. Districts that take great pains to nurture community connections both initiate and sustain OBE implementation with greater success.

2) The system transformation approach to OBE gives an exciting new slant to the terms outcomes, purpose, focus, learning, and performance that brings staff together, enhances professionalism, redefines many different aspects of teaching and assessing, and gives students the motivation and responsibility to work hard and perform well.

3) OBE unleashes the potential for success that is inherent in

schools, staff, students, and their communities. The more that schools and communities focus on outcomes and abilities that go beyond traditional schoolwork itself, the more exciting, motivating, and powerful are the learning experiences that get developed and implemented.

4) Both "transformational" and "traditional" approaches to defining and accomplishing outcomes can co-exist. Time and again, students in settings that challenge them to engage in difficult, life-relevant projects also do better in typical academic skills and endeavors. Role performances enhance and extend academic learning, not replace it, and the data from several districts stand as proof.

5) It all comes down to performance and the ability of educators to clearly define what constitutes the components of a quality performance. When they can do that and teach their students how performance criteria and the frameworks for those criteria (rubrics) work, the students will take it from there on their own and have an invaluable, lifelong tool.

Chapter 6
Why All the Controversy About OBE?

Although most had never heard the term Outcome-Based Education before 1990, today millions are hearing or reading about it in all forms of the mass media. OBE is now a widely discussed topic from local PTA and school board meetings to state legislative debates and national radio talk shows. In comparison to the information presented in Chapters 1 through 5, most of the things people hear or read about OBE from the media are serious misrepresentations of what authentic OBE actually is. Unfortunately, these misconceptions fuel criticism and organized political opposition to OBE as well as promote further confusion and misunderstanding.

When critics and opposition groups speak out, they use one label — OBE — to argue against a variety of diverse, sometimes unrelated improvement-oriented reforms. Some concerns seem to be based on ideology and values, some on poor implementation practices, others on fear of change, and yet others on the specter of unwanted political control. Regardless of the reasons, the OBE label has become the lightning rod for all these concerns, and state education leaders and policy officials, local school board members and administrators, and classroom implementers are all holding the rod.

Consequently, the purpose of this chapter is to address explicitly the criticisms being leveled against both "real" and "imagined" OBE so that many existing misunderstandings and misrepresentations can be laid to rest. This should allow a set of common understandings and agreements to emerge, from which educators, parents, community leaders, and policymakers can safely and soundly proceed.

1. Who are the groups that have taken a stance against outcome-based reforms?

Outside of the education system, those registering some degree of opposition to OBE seem to fall into three broad, overlapping categories: activist opponents, vocal critics, and concerned individuals. While active opposition has surfaced in many state capitals and local communities, it seems to be fueled by the publications and/or organizing efforts of several prominent national organizations, including Pat Robertson's Christian Coalition, Robert Simonds' Citizens for Excellence in Education, Phyllis Schlafly's Eagle Forum, Beverly La Haye's Concerned Women for America, and the Rutherford Institute. Several prominent conservative leaders, media personalities, and politicians fall into the category of being vocal critics of what they understand OBE to be. Besides the individuals just mentioned, they include former U.S. Secretary of Education William Bennett, media personalities Rush Limbaugh and G. Gordon Liddy, and commentator and former presidential candidate Pat Buchanan.

The third group consists of citizens and parents who are often influenced by the things these other individuals say.

2. Are these organized groups actually united in their opposition to OBE?

While pro and con opinions and declarations on this issue vary, what is quite apparent is the tenacity of their opposition to what might be called "progressive reforms" and the enormous amount of data, information, and misinformation that is shared among the different groups listed in the previous question. National, state, and local newsletters from various conservative and religious organizations abound — often repeating exactly the same stories with the same inaccuracies over a period of months. Since late 1992, critics have regularly shared this information and their viewpoints widely with all forms of the media.

In addition, some opposition groups have effectively drawn each other's members to protest rallies and to local and state school board meetings — often busing hundreds of people into local meetings from a substantial distance. Educators report seeing the same OBE opponents attend meetings in community after community, frequently claiming to be members of that particular community.

3. What do these opponents and critics hope to accomplish by derailing outcome-based reform efforts?

While educators and journalists have puzzled extensively over this question, the documents produced by opposition groups, coupled with statements their leaders make in public forums, have led to all kinds of public conjecture, which those leaders generally deny. The most prominent conjectures include:

1) Reducing the influence of state and federal governments over local educational policies and programs.

2) Reversing the growing influence of internationalist and global thinking in both curriculum and politics.

3) Eliminating all "New Age" philosophical influences and practices from the public school curriculum and in society at large.

4) Restoring in our social, political, and educational institutions the pro-Christian philosophy they believe the Founding Fathers intended the nation to embody.

5) Taking over the local school boards — some to achieve desired representation, others as a first step to controlling the political and philosophical agenda of the country.

6) Establishing a powerful grass-roots political organization to shape local, state, and national electoral results and policy agendas.

7) Preventing the public schools from what they see as diluting the traditional emphasis on individual excellence for the purpose of an unjustified emphasis on egalitarianism.

8) Preventing the public schools from improving, thereby strengthening arguments for private school alternatives and tax-supported voucher systems.

The rationale underlying several of these possibilities will be explained later in the chapter.

4. What about outcome-based reforms do these organized groups find objectionable?

There are two aspects to this question. On the one hand, their list of objections includes numerous things that have nothing directly to do with OBE, but which run counter to their philosophy — sex education, global studies, and ungraded classrooms among them. OBE frequently gets used as the catch-all label for all "progressive" educational practices and reforms. During 1994, the breadth of this "OBE umbrella" extended to the halls of the U.S. Congress where the critics fought to block the reauthorization of the Elementary and Secondary Education Act and the passage of the administration's Goals 2000 initiative — both of which they labeled outcome-based.

Of the issues that are directly related to OBE, concerns and criticisms seem to revolve around nine distinct, but interrelated, themes:

1) What outcomes are

2) Substance versus symbolism

3) What OBE is

4) Governmental control and accountability

5) Philosophy and world view

6) Cost versus effectiveness

7) Proven versus experimental

8) Standards versus success

9) Instructional opportunities.

While disentangling any single theme or issue from the others is diffi-cult, we will address each issue with the intent of clarifying what is being disputed. This information should help dispel the misunderstandings sur-rounding outcome-based reforms and establish some common ground among the OBE proponents and opponents. As suggested in Chapters 3 through 5, OBE offers a lot of what the critics want but currently misun-derstand, including traditional implementation models that match their strongest preferences.

5. Should parents, taxpayers, policymakers, and educators be concerned about these nine issues?

Yes! OBE and its implementation should be given thoughtful examina-tion by anyone it directly or indirectly affects. Given OBE's major implications for total system change, parents and the public should care-fully scrutinize and discuss all nine of these issues. The problem, which OBE advocates continue to point out, is that until late 1994, the public was hearing only one side of the controversy, largely because the oppo-nents and critics waged a dedicated media campaign. Either inadvertent-ly or, in some cases perhaps intentionally, this campaign selectively and persistently distorted and misrepresented the body of evidence that defines what OBE is and stands for. This chapter intends to explain each issue in its own right and set the record straight about OBE's actual meaning, intention, power, and potential.

6. What's the controversy about "what outcomes are?"

Of all the issues, this is by far the most important since almost everything else emanates from it. The heart of the problem seems to be twofold. First, some examples of "outcomes" as defined and applied in the field directly embody aspects of personal values and psychological states that OBE oppo-nents and critics find objectionable. Although Chapters 1 and 3 explain that examples of that kind fall outside the boundaries of a properly defined and operationalized outcome, they exist nonetheless. Many educators and poli-cymakers openly advocate them, especially those related to tolerance toward others, positive self-concept, and achievement motivation. To make matters worse, critics have identified many of these examples, pointing to them as the embodiment of OBE's intentions and substantive agenda. Whether properly defined or not, some states and districts include these kinds of out-come statements within their outcome frameworks.

Second, compounding the problem of defining these kinds of real outcome statements is the major misinterpretation of what "transformational" outcomes are. We have verified through numerous of conversations that many leading OBE opponents actually believe that transformational outcomes 1) are nothing but values and psychological states and 2) deliberately ignore academic content. How these misunderstandings arose is not the issue; that they are so pervasive, deeply felt, and believed is of great concern.

For whatever reason, critics have come to view and represent many states' and local districts' outcomes as "transformational," which to them means "transforming the values, attitudes, and psychological frames of mind of students into something the state desires." As incorrect as this allegation appears, it nonetheless interprets and portrays outcomes as only being these affective states. Hence, the opposition's reasoning goes, since outcomes drive curriculum, instruction, and assessment, schools will have to abandon "critical knowledge" and "measurable competence" in favor of these "fuzzy, affective" factors. Based on these assertions, critics further contend that under OBE, students will only be tested and graded on their social values, attitudes, personalities, and behaviors. Furthermore, there is every reason to expect that as long as opponents believe that OBE is deliberately advocating specific values, attitudes, and psychological states of mind as its substantive agenda, they will remain opposed to anything resembling this approach to education.

What can be done? What can those who advocate OBE do about this very serious and fundamental problem? Two things seem obvious. First, they must work with their colleagues and carefully scrutinize everything they have developed that might be construed as an outcome and examine its wording against the criteria, definitions, and examples provided in Chapter 3. If it is not a clearly defined demonstration of learning, or if the demonstration presumes that the learner is to advocate some explicit personal value, then the item in question is a prime candidate for modification or abandonment. Possibly, community consensus about "civic goals" that schools should pursue may be reached, while keeping "personal values" out of outcome demonstrations altogether.

Second, educators must reach out to everyone in their state, district, and community interested in education and explain the issues surrounding outcomes of significance again and again with the clearest examples possible. Many OBE critics are absolutely certain of their position on this matter, and it may take repeated efforts to set the definition and implementation record straight. It will be particularly important to show Figure 3.1 (the "Outcome Aliases") as many times as necessary and to be able to explain exactly why each of the 12 aliases is there. The more educators can reinforce the reality that outcomes are demonstrated results, the sooner the widespread misunderstandings will dissipate.

Also critical to this second point is Figure 3.5, the Demonstration Mountain. The major issue there is to establish the meaning of the top sector of the mountain and what kind of demonstrations it represents. This will require separating the notion of having learners demonstrate complex role performance abilities from having them advocate any particular personal or social value or attitude.

Related to this issue is the easily misunderstood "BE LIKE" term in Figure 3.2, the Learning Performance Pyramid. OBE implementers must be prepared to explain in a variety of ways that the often misinterpreted "BE LIKE" term is about the constellation of confidence and motivation issues that make successful performances possible — not that OBE implementers want students to "be like" a particular person or have a given kind of personality.

The matter of testing and grading students on "inappropriate outcomes" is another concern. Basically, those with extensive experience in implementing OBE have never advocated testing or grading students on the substance of either their personal values or the positions they take in discussions or debates. (If such practices exist, they should stop, OBE or not.) Consequently, OBE makes a sharp distinction between students' personal views and how well they can explain the strengths and weaknesses of particular arguments or conclusions drawn from available evidence. For decades, educators have viewed the latter as a legitimate component of critical thinking and complex problem-solving abilities. In a similar vein, those who implement OBE also separate personal and religious values that are individual matters from those broad civic values — such as honesty, integrity, and fairness — that make stable, democratic, community living possible.

Some inroads made. One of the most encouraging signs in this whole area of outcomes is to hear some OBE critics making distinctions among different kinds of outcomes and lending support to those that match their educational priorities. This is a major step forward from what has been a blanket condemnation of all outcomes simply because they are called "outcomes."

7. What's the controversy about "substance versus symbolism" in OBE?

Closely related to the controversy about what outcomes are is whether they have real substance or are simply symbolic "fluff." Because the most vocal OBE opponents perceive outcomes as soft and fuzzy attitudes, values, and psychological states of mind, their logic leads them to conclude that outcomes lack real substance. Minus substance and the scores and grades that go with it, they claim OBE is nothing more than an empty shell advocating "success for all," but on things that can't be defined or measured and that schools shouldn't be messing with anyway.

Experienced OBE implementers readily acknowledge that values, attitudes, and psychological states represented by terms like "self-concept" and "tolerance" are not outcomes and cannot be measured the way authentic performances can. Moreover, with their definition of an outcome as a foundation, they interpret and describe the substance versus symbolism issue in exactly the opposite way as do the critics.

The key to understanding this highly charged issue is to focus on the substance of a learning demonstration. To do so requires identifying:

- The substance of what is to be demonstrated

- The process the learner is to carry out

- The setting or circumstances under which the demonstrating is to be done.

In an authentic outcome-based approach, implementers would focus on the clearly defined substance of all three dimensions. For example 1) "the battles of the Civil War" are totally different from "the Bill of Rights," even though both are important components of American history; 2) the process of "listing" either of them is totally different from the process of "explaining" them; and 3) "at a classroom seat with a piece of paper" is totally different from "before an audience of American history experts."

To carry this thinking even further, the teachers of these potential outcomes would be asked to define clearly for their students and themselves the components needed in the student's demonstration of the defined outcome. To do this the scope and accuracy of the content must be defined, as well as the key elements in the required processes demonstrating the outcome. Teachers would then make sure they explicitly taught all these components, gave the students needed practice and feedback in carrying them out, and designed an assessment that perfectly matched and embodied the defined outcome. In other words, the hallmark of an outcome-based approach is clarity and consistency in defining what is substantive and important and not confusing substance with scores and grades.

As mentioned in Chapter 2, excellent examples of this type of criterion-based performance system are merit and honor badges in the Boy and Girl Scouts. These badges are defined totally by substance and clear performance components. They have no scores, no letter grades, and no averages — just clear criteria like well-defined outcomes do. Furthermore, in the Scouts and in OBE, you are called "done" and "successful" when you have demonstrated *all* of those criterion components to a high standard. Anything less puts you in the "In Progress/Keep Trying" category. Note the Scouts don't have the C, D, F, or "Remedial" categories that schools have created for students who are not consistently successful the first time they attempt something.

From this strong substantive perspective, scores and grades are not accurate measures of student learning — substantive criteria are! True, people are accustomed to viewing and treating scores and grades as if they were the actual achievements of students. But experienced OBE implementers recognize that grades and scores are simply artifacts and byproducts of the assessment and evaluation process teachers use. This familiar process is summarized in Figure 2.4 of Chapter 2, "The Five Great Illusions of Achievement." Traditional assessment and evaluation assumes that all performances are inherently worth 100 points and that you should treat all points (which really means all parts of the learning demonstration) as if they were equal and perfectly interchangeable. From a substantive point of view, neither is true.

The process further assumes that if students cannot do something, the instructor should simply take off an appropriate number of points. In most systems, 70 points is good enough to have the performance considered acceptable — but imagine what that would mean in the case of what is considered acceptable driving. From a criterion-based perspective, this could translate into millions of automobile accidents per hour on America's highways. Finally, the ultimate illusion is that the more points students pile up, the more learning and achievement they have, which completely disregards the major substantive differences in genuine learning demonstrations as well as the critical difference between initial practice and ultimate performance ability. That is why OBE implementers often say:

> As substance, grades mean nothing!
> As symbols, grades mean everything!

The irony is that OBE offers parents and educators a much more substantive definition and picture of students' learning than anything our current system offers. And OBE further reminds us that true measures are not about scores and percents, but about clearly defined criteria. When those criteria are clearly present in a student's performance, he or she has met the standard. When they are not all present, the performance is incomplete and needs to be improved. That shifts the definition of learning and achievement from "getting points" to "consistently doing high quality work." A lot of people haven't understood this shift yet, but it's the backbone of defining and accomplishing quality learning — something that both OBE advocates and critics want badly.

Those with extensive OBE experience readily recognize that 1) grades and scores disguise the actual substance of learning, and 2) students with quite dissimilar patterns of performance could easily end up with the same final score, which provides neither them nor their teacher with a clear indicator of what they need to do to improve their learning and subsequent performance. So, the major irony is that implementing OBE actually reverses the "substance versus symbols" equation as the critics portray it. OBE is focused on real substance, but the traditional system is awash in vague symbols!

8. What's the controversy about "what OBE is?"

Much of the controversy and misunderstanding about OBE is caused by and is inseparable from the controversies surrounding outcomes and substance versus symbolism. Therefore, clarifying what OBE is requires clarifying the other two issues first. Once that is done, attention should turn to describing and explaining what defines an outcome-based system and how it differs from conventional practice, which means relying heavily on the frameworks and issues developed in Chapters 1, 2, and 4. Chapters 1 and 4 make clear what OBE is and isn't; Chapter 2 differentiates 10 OBE components from those of the current system. These definitions, components, and realities have been conspicuously absent from the critics' public portrayal of OBE.

Like their representation of outcomes, the critics' portrayal of OBE has been to find the weakest, most objectionable examples of a broad array of practices or designs they or others call OBE, then to use those worst-case examples to characterize what all of OBE is and advocates. While it is natural to expect dedicated critics of any idea or approach to focus on its weakest examples and most negative possibilities, in the case of OBE, the critics' representation:

- Badly distorts what outcomes are.

- Treats the four different faces of OBE discussed in Chapter 4 as if they were the same thing.

- Ignores or badly misrepresents OBE's two purposes and four principles.

- Finds only fault in what schools and districts have done to implement those purposes and principles.

- Includes countless things that are only peripherally associated with OBE.

The overwhelming impression these perspectives give is that OBE is a collection of weak and dangerous practices driven by the worst of political or social intentions.

Finding common ground. So where does one begin establishing a common ground for productive dialogue? In the same place that we begin discussing outcomes, by:

- Acknowledging that poor examples exist and need to be changed or eliminated.

- Continually emphasizing clear definitions of outcomes, criterion standards, and OBE's guiding purposes and principles.

- Clarifying the distinctly different configurations of OBE implementation.

- Repeatedly emphasizing the need for greater clarity, common sense, and effectiveness in the current system.

- Continuing to reference the models and practices in the field that exemplify the power and potential inherent in OBE.

Again, growing evidence suggests that some of the major opponents and critics of OBE want to establish a dialogue around these issues because they want the existing system to improve as much as OBE advocates do. Where to begin? A good place to start is by practicing the fundamentals just described and continuing to reference the frameworks, definitions, and examples provided in Chapters 1 through 5 — especially "The OBE Pyramid" in Figure 1.2 of Chapter 1 and the results described throughout Chapter 5.

9. What's the controversy about "governmental control and accountability"?

Without question, the active role that states and the federal government have played in the early '90s to spur school reform at the local level accounts for a great amount of the reaction against what the opposition is calling OBE. They see the worst of motives and the worst of potential consequences in these governmental initiatives, partly because of what they regard as their objectionable substance and partly because they inherently view the government as interfering inappropriately in local and family matters that involve values and beliefs. For better and certainly for worse, these state and federal reform initiatives have become wedded to the term OBE and, true or not, each gets blamed for embodying what are viewed as the other's worst aspects.

Although very few governmental initiatives meet the criteria of a true outcome-based approach, anything resembling or associated with defining and assessing performance goals runs the risk of being portrayed as both OBE and governmental interference simultaneously. While many opponents agree on their distrust and dislike of the federal government (and the federal initiative Goals 2000), they also allege that states have overstepped their bounds by forcing students to learn and demonstrate particular things as conditions for graduation. Both are seen as part of the larger OBE "problem."

Two major dimensions characterize this issue. First, authentic OBE has always been a local matter. Throughout the '70s and '80s, OBE implementation was almost exclusively handled, without major political incident, by district boards of education and district staff. Outcomes focused on established programs and curricula, and district staffs were granted the authority to define and implement them based on their expertise as educators. However, when the more future-focused and life-context oriented "transformational" approach to OBE began to evolve in the late '80s, those who facilitated its implementation insisted on having extensive community involvement in the mission-setting and outcome-defining processes of each district. That sensible and effective practice is followed today more than ever.

Community input and support are essential to the success of OBE implementation from both a substantive and political perspective. Over the past several years, the strategic design process mentioned in Chapters 3, 4, and 5 has directly involved large numbers of community stakeholders in OBE direction-setting and design processes. It has set a strong precedent for large-scale community involvement within districts wishing to pursue future-focused role performance outcomes. This high level of community outreach and participation directly contradicts the assertion that OBE is inherently driven by state or federal governmental bodies and desires to circumvent local priorities and input.

The second key dimension of this governmental control issue involves a major paradox: Namely, under almost all current state laws and regulations, it is almost impossible for any local district to become genuinely outcome-based. Why? Because state policies regarding the accreditation of schools and the credentialing of students are all based on time definitions and time requirements and are unrelated to clear definitions of student learning results. OBE implementers have always had to deal with the reality that everything in our Industrial Age educational system is legally constituted and regulated to last a specific amount of time (usually nine months on the dot). School years, curriculum structures, courses, Carnegie units of credit, promotion processes, funding, and teacher contracts are all prime examples. Since schooling and graduation are measured by their time and resource inputs, not their outcomes, these time-based regulations have seriously constrained the implementation of authentic OBE at the district level, largely because the locals need time flexibility to make OBE work optimally. Local districts that tried to become fully outcome-based couldn't because they always had rigid, state-enforced calendars and credentialing schedules staring them in the face. So many of them have had to make the best compromises within these institutional constraints.

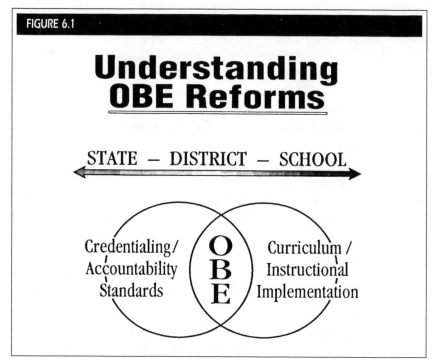

FIGURE 6.1

Understanding OBE Reforms

STATE − DISTRICT − SCHOOL

Credentialing/ Accountability Standards

O B E

Curriculum / Instructional Implementation

The essence of this dilemma is illustrated by Figure 6.1. There we see two intersecting circles representing what it takes to have a genuinely outcome-based system. One circle is credentialing and accountability standards based on outcomes, not a nine-month calendar.

Similarly, the other is a curriculum and instructional implementation system based on the same outcomes, not the nine-month calendar. What the picture indicates is that local schools and states have been at an institutional stalemate over these two critical subsystems for most of the century. Schools control the curriculum and instructional subsystem, and many of them have wanted to become outcome based. They haven't been able to because the state controls how curriculum and instruction translate into graduation requirements and credits, and, until recently, the latter two have been wholly time based.

The paradox in this dilemma is that as some states are acting to put more substance into their graduation standards and even giving local districts discretion in defining them in performance terms, they are being accused of overstepping their legal authority. This particular accusation is inappropriate because states have always had jurisdiction over credentialing and accountability standards. It seems, instead, that what they are really overstepping is the boundary of accepted social convention, which is very hard to alter. After all, everyone who's been to school knows what a Carnegie unit is (120 hours of seat time in a course), and that you must accumulate 22 of them to graduate. But who's ever seen or agreed with a clear, criterion-based performance standard, especially one that is supposed to apply to all students? The answer is anyone who has spent time reading and applying the Boy Scout and Girl Scout manuals, for one.

A further paradox is that the federal government's attempt to define national standards in the core curriculum areas as part of its Goals 2000 initiative is not really outcome-based, it is curriculum-based. The standards are being formed around the traditional subject areas that have defined the American high school since 1893. The standards and the assessments that accompany them almost certainly will reinforce the existing separation of the subject areas and limit the student performances to structured tasks and discrete content skills (those found in the bottom half of the Demonstration Mountain in Figure 3.5 of Chapter 3). Although this hardly seems like a major departure from what schools have always done, if enacted, national standards would leave local citizens and educators out of the outcome-defining process and inherently limit their curricular options.

10. What's the controversy about "philosophy and world view" in OBE?

Underlying a great deal of the controversy over OBE are what have been expressed as major differences in viewpoints about children, families, schooling, and other social and political institutions. Those who advocate and implement OBE have a very optimistic viewpoint about children and their ability to accomplish great things when inspired and challenged appropriately. But as a group, they view some of the traditional structures of our public education system more skeptically, largely because they recognize in them major rigidities and constraints that seriously limit what educators and students can accomplish. As explained in Chapter 2, OBE supporters see the system as having served the purposes and needs of the Industrial Age very well, but they recognize change is imperative. The challenges facing America in the Information Age require different outcomes of students and their schools, different curricula, different instructional approaches and learning environments, and different patterns of success.

By contrast, the viewpoint of some of OBE's most organized and vocal critics seems to reflect a tremendous respect, if not reverence, for these same traditional characteristics. In general, the critics are highly conservative politically, and they openly oppose changes in what they regard to be those things about the system that are clearly understood. This includes the system's existing structures, curriculum focus, emphasis on competition, and differentiation of talent and opportunities. Critics interpret these familiar characteristics as both desirable and inherently "American." Consequently, what education reformers of all kinds offer as badly needed changes and sometimes describe in unfamiliar and nebulous terminology, many of the critics view as "ambiguous," "nonacademic," and "dangerous," and openly resist.

Red-flag terms. The list of things these groups have opposed includes: outcomes; anything called outcome-based, performance-based, or results-based; national standards of any kind; cooperative learning; collaborative projects; learning teams; integrated curriculum; critical thinking; constructivist thinking; social responsibility; social interaction; attitudes and values; tolerance; human psychology and development; personal wellness; ungraded classrooms or schools; multiage grouping; flexible grouping; flexible scheduling; year-round schooling; authentic assessments; performance portfolios; computer-based record-keeping; anything multicultural; whole language instruction; learning styles; anything global; and site-based management.

At one level, it appears this list includes virtually everything that isn't a manifestation of the most traditional aspects of schooling, which leaves little room for agreeing about major system change. At another, it is simply inaccurate to include all these things in a clearly defined picture of what an OBE system actually is. Many of these concepts have little or no direct relationship to the definitions and frameworks discussed in Chapters 1 through 4. Finally, unfortunately some critics have gone so far as to label all these things with terms such as New Age, global, internationalist, socialist, unAmerican, humanist, occult, satanic, anti-Christian, and politically correct. These labels only add to the confusion and controversy, and thus misrepresent the substantive issues around which a common ground might be built.

For a deeper understanding of the philosophy and world view underlying much of the opposition to OBE, one is best advised to carefully read the articles by Robert Marzanno and Robert Simonds in the January 1994 issue of *Educational Leadership*, and by Arnold Burron in the March 1994 issue. Marzanno explicitly details the basis of some critics' anti-"New Age" perspectives. He lists a host of individuals, institutions, and everyday practices that have been labeled by those whose thinking seems to embody the views of a vocal segment of OBE opponents.

Marzanno suggests the term New Age is used to characterize almost anything that seems to depart from what he describes as an "ultra-fundamentalist" world view — one that has a number of connections to what Burron identifies in his article as a "Traditionalist Christian" philosophy.

The Simonds article conveys the thinking, motivation, and goals of one of the most nationally visible OBE critics. Simonds and his Citizens for Excellence in Education colleagues have been responsible for providing their constituents across the country with information and strategies to criticize what they find objectionable about the range of outcome-based reforms just mentioned. While Simonds has expressed publicly his general agreement with the direction and nature of "Traditional OBE," his objections increase with the more complex performances and applications (depicted as the higher one climbs the Demonstration Mountain shown in Chapter 3). In general, he sees in OBE the potential for state interference in matters he regards as the exclusive purview of the family — especially in its advocacy of values and attitudes that depart from his Christian beliefs. Simonds' goals are to raise learning standards, increase the responsiveness of school systems to parent input, and protect the interests of children. Ironically, these aims sound identical to those of OBE's strongest adherents!

Burron's article is useful for illustrating two major beliefs that underlie what he calls Traditionalist Christian philosophy. Adherents of this philosophy object to many of the values and the affective agenda they see manifested in state and local outcome frameworks. This is partially because of their belief in "supersessionalism" — the view that their interpretation of Christianity is above all other religions. This belief underlies their opposition to classroom representations of Christianity, which they believe impose upon their children the burden of espousing a "politically correct," "unitarian," or "universalist" philosophy to avoid social or academic ostracizing.

The second Traditionalist Christian fundamental belief is that the family is the tangible embodiment of God's connection to the church, with the husband holding the superordinate position and the wife serving as his helpmate. Any viewpoint that suggests this hierarchical relationship between the sexes should be altered is "diametrically opposed" to this belief and, it appears, is understood and treated as an example of New Age philosophy.

As the attempt to build a common ground proceeds, it is essential to recognize that not all OBE critics share a similar religious or philosophical outlook — they do not. But critics do seem united in their view that anything other than patriotism and devotion to traditional institutions can be explicit threats to our children's and nation's well-being.

11. What's the controversy about "cost versus effectiveness" in OBE?

In their attempt to discredit all aspects of OBE, many critics have claimed that it has a track record of costly failures. One of their key arguments is that valid "research" proving it works is lacking. Similarly, critics allege that states and districts have spent and/or wasted huge sums of money on OBE efforts and have nothing to show for it. When these two arguments are put together, their question is: Who would ever want to pursue OBE in the first place?

The answer is many schools and districts were attracted to OBE partly by its philosophy, but mainly by the successes others were having with whatever form of "OBE" they were using at the time. Chapter 5 lists these districts and schools and outlines their efforts.

But here's the rub: OBE's critics and opponents regularly claim "independent, nationally validated, systematic research" proving that OBE works does not exist. Without national research, they claim, "convincing proof" is absent. Furthermore, they assert that locally collected data are simply "self-serving propaganda." On these three points, they are one-third right.

Although there is a large body of research literature on Mastery Learning (which applies to only a few of these nationally recognized examples), no one in the educational research community has designed and carried out a major study of the effectiveness other less well-known OBE models. Documenting results of such a study would be enormously challenging, because determining what aspects of OBE were or weren't making a difference on what kinds of outcomes would vary a great deal from model to model. Consequently, the only available data about these historical and contemporary examples are what local educators have collected themselves — in some cases with painstaking care.

Compounding the controversy of OBE's effectiveness is 1) the critics' emphasis on various state and local OBE examples they call "failures," and 2) their claim that these negative examples characterize the whole of OBE. Our experience suggests the vast majority of examples they cite falls far short of embodying the criteria of authentic outcome-based implementation. Consequently, critics often judge and characterize OBE through weak and inappropriate examples, while OBE's proponents do just the opposite.

In addition, the critics' allegations about the extreme costs of implementing OBE do not match up against the budget realities of major OBE implementation. The huge discrepancies between what the critics claim the costs are or will be and what implementing schools or districts actually have spent on outcome-based strategic planning, staff development, and program development cannot be reconciled.

However, one possible explanation for these grossly inflated cost estimates is that they may be based on extrapolations some states have made to develop, test, and administer new statewide assessment systems, which the critics think of as OBE. Without question, these costs can be quite high in total dollars, but state or national assessments generally are not considered necessary or particularly useful parts of an OBE system. Nor are they a part of local district budgets.

All of the schools and districts described in Chapter 5 implemented OBE and accomplished what they did:

- Within the bounds of their existing budgets.

- Because they wanted to locally.

- Without any kind of expensive state or national assessment to support their efforts.

Therefore, while it is appropriate for critics to point out what these large-scale assessment costs may be, it is inappropriate to associate them with necessary local expenditures or operating costs.

However, anyone considering the potential costs of OBE or any other significant systemic reform must consider two major factors. First, to implement a fully developed OBE model at the local level will require significant retraining of personnel; redesign of the system; and retooling of its curriculum, instruction, assessment, and credentialing components. While these front-end costs will not be cheap, they can be phased in over time as an investment in overhauling a system that 1) is not meeting the needs of many of its students and tax-paying clients, 2) is tied to many Industrial Age precedents and procedures, and 3) has operated without significant change for nearly a century. Even earmarking an annual 1 percent of the typical operating budget for fundamental retooling can make a huge difference in how the system operates and how well students learn.

Second, experienced OBE administrators consistently report that day-to-day costs for operating a highly effective OBE school or district are no higher than operating a less effective, traditional one. But OBE does require wiser allocation of available funds, resources, and personnel — which many successful implementers are happy to describe to those interested. The practitioners cited in Chapter 5 were eager to focus the public's attention on OBE's cost versus effectiveness, since the comparison makes OBE look like a stunning alternative to what we are getting from the current system. To tax-conscious citizens, OBE may be the best educational bargain on the block. To the students, parents, and educators who have directly experienced its benefits, it is absolutely worth the investment.

12. What's the controversy about what's "proven versus experimental" in OBE?

This seventh controversial issue is strongly linked to the one just discussed and to the initial issue: What are outcomes? Many critics and opponents claim OBE is "unproven" and no systematic research documents its effectiveness. At a generic level this charge is groundless since the world is filled with OBE examples (Figure 1.1 of Chapter 1). These examples obviously work, or they would have been replaced with something else long ago. At a more specific level, however, the allegation is being made about OBE "in schools," which invites and requires a more in-depth response.

First, to implement anything that represents a major departure from business as usual is going to take considerable time, and the variations in how well and how willingly people do it are generally very great. For this reason, the press for quality control and the impetus toward continuous improvement being undertaken in American business and industry (see Chapter 2) is both very critical and long-range in scope. The fundamental assumption of the giants in the quality field, like the late W. Edwards Deming, is that people and systems will continue to be imperfect. The objective, then, is to get stakeholders committed to identifying the sources of the imperfection and continuing to narrow the range between the best and worst cases of anything — always bringing the worst closer and closer to the best.

Buy-in varies. In terms of OBE implementation in schools, the scope and rate of change inevitably will be uneven. Some teachers may never fully or even partially exercise its principles and philosophy in their classrooms. Consequently, the best overall gains are disproportionately seen in the individual schools or whole districts of the more advanced implementers, and would be even greater if everyone were equally as involved. In the few cases where districts have studied the effects of implementation differences, the achievement levels of students in "high implementation" OBE classes have been much higher than in "low" or "no" implementation settings.

Second, given the nature and culture of school systems, the matter of "proven" has two very different meanings. The first relates to the practical standards of practitioners. Overall, practitioners are not always consumers of formal educational research, and highly technical statistical reports leave them with little sense of what to do practically. When practitioners do use research, the studies they consider mostly deal with the explicit responsibilities and situations they face on a daily basis. What "proven" generally means to them is that something is convincing based on evidence they can observe. When this evidence comes by example or demonstration from a practitioner who has successfully faced similar challenges it is even more credible. Consequently, workshops and presentations at local, regional, and national OBE conferences featuring concrete examples from practitioners at the schools and districts mentioned earlier have been widely accepted as "proof" that OBE works.

The second meaning of "proven" — the more rigorous scientific one the critics embrace — is simply much less important and convincing to practitioners. Consequently, they are less interested in and less convinced by precisely determined statistics than by a clear "show me" demonstration of what something is and how it works. This is not to argue that rigorous studies of OBE efforts should not be done — quite the contrary. OBE advocates would have been delighted had the educational research community paid more attention to their examples as they unfolded, but no one did. That has meant OBE practitioners have had to depend on the self-evaluations and internally focused studies just cited. However, a number of districts in the early stages of major implementation efforts — like Mooresville, North Carolina; Syracuse, New York; and Yarmouth, Maine — would benefit enormously from "process research" undertaken to document their results. These systems are seeking researchers to document their efforts.

Finally, OBE's critics and opponents have given a particularly negative cast to the term "experimental," implying uncontrolled and irresponsible action is taking place in schools. Moreover, they say these actions are intended to shape or warp the thinking, beliefs, and values of students and that their consequences cannot be predicted. To a large degree, this argument is linked to the assertion that outcomes are nothing but values, attitudes, and psychological states of mind and, therefore, OBE classrooms must be manipulating children's minds in dangerous ways — an assertion explicitly rejected in this book. There is simply no evidence of this kind of psychological manipulation in any of the schools and districts that have been key examples of OBE implementation in the field.

How much better to have the tenor of this issue shift from "experimental" to "innovative," which implies educators are deliberately trying out and applying promising new ideas and approaches to see how well they can make them work. That, we find, has been the guiding spirit of the OBE practices with the greatest impact on the field.

13. What's the controversy about "standards versus success" in OBE?

This eighth controversial issue is based on an understandable but incorrect assumption: Because OBE insists on creating success for all students, it does so by lowering standards to a level that the poorest students can reach. This, the critics claim, leads to "dumbing down" the curriculum and to impeding the opportunities for greater challenge and advancement that higher achieving students deserve and should receive.

In fact, the opposite is true. OBE always has stood for high expectations as well as high standards for all students. The influential examples in the previous chapter embrace that commitment. Serious advocates of outcome-based efforts object to lowering either standards or expectations for what students can eventually accomplish. Instead, they consistently work toward raising the expectations and performance levels for what students can do by systematically, creatively, and simultaneously applying OBE's four power principles to what they do.

But the critics' assumption about lowering standards has a definite logic — a logic grounded in the dynamics surrounding achievement and success, portrayed in Figure 6.2, "The Fixed Commodity Paradigm of Achievement." The essence of this paradigm is that standards and success are bound to each other in a fixed, reciprocal, closed-system relationship, much like a teeter-totter. The paradigm assumes two major things. First, the availability and effectiveness of instructional support cannot be altered (or is irrelevant to how much is achieved). Second, only a fixed, finite supply of achievement is available within the system, and it is acquired either by raising standards, therefore lowering the number who succeed, or by raising the likelihood of success by lowering the standard.

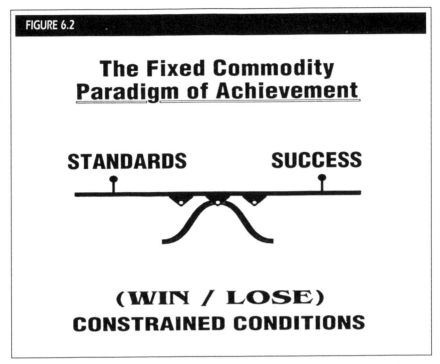

FIGURE 6.2

The Fixed Commodity Paradigm of Achievement

STANDARDS   **SUCCESS**

(WIN / LOSE) CONSTRAINED CONDITIONS

The paradigm reflects a classic competitive, win/lose orientation to learning and achievement: For every win there must be a corresponding loss simply because the conditions under which the game is played — calendar-defined schedule, constrained opportunity, competitive environment, and comparative evaluation — are defined to create that result. In addition, those conditions are compounded by delivering instruction according to the traditional assembly-line approach of "everyone doing exactly the same thing at the same time." Under these opportunity conditions, anyone who can't keep up with the assembly-line schedule is virtually assured of "losing."

But beyond these conditions, the competitive orientation of many critics is linked to a deep-seated belief in the merits of capitalism and the critical role that a competitive orientation plays in capitalistic success. To weaken this competitive urge, argue the critics, is to weaken capitalistic energy, which, in their view, is an invitation to allow socialism to emerge.

Both parts of this argument are the opposite of what OBE strives to achieve. Instead of the teeter-totter, OBE implementation is guided by the metaphor of a criterion-based, learning and achievement elevator powered by OBE's four principles (see Figure 6.3). The elevator represents what we

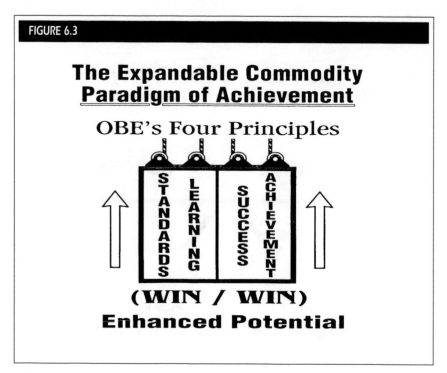

call "The Expandable Commodity Paradigm of Achievement" — a paradigm that assumes that learning, achievement, standards, and success are not balanced and pitted against each other in a win/lose dynamic but can be expanded and elevated through the power of effective interventions linked to their consistent, systematic, creative, and simultaneous application.

OBE's four principles transform the win/lose dynamic of the teeter-totter into the win/win dynamic of the elevator. No one must lose in order for others to win. Rather, all can win on their own terms in relation to a clearly defined set of challenging performance criteria. This combination of factors is used in OBE classrooms to raise the levels of achievements and challenge for all students without impeding the progress of faster or slower students. OBE teachers frequently report observing most of their students advancing far beyond their own previous levels and those of equivalent groups of students in previous years.

The crux of this dilemma is that OBE can raise standards and raise levels of challenge for students to do better without having to resort to win/lose competition to achieve higher results for each individual student. From the critics' point of view, this is neither logical, possible, nor desirable.

14. What's the controversy about "instructional opportunities" in OBE?

This final issue is strongly related to the previous one, because both are based on assumptions about the conditions that define and affect classroom instruction. The critics contend that, in its desire to "equalize" the achievements of all students, OBE delivery retards the pace and level of instruction to match that of the lowest/slowest learners. In doing so, they argue, it both "dumbs down" the curriculum and compels faster, more advanced students to spend their time helping their lower, less motivated peers at the expense of advancing their own learning. These concerns are linked to three things: 1) OBE's expanded opportunity principle, 2) the use of various cooperative learning strategies by some OBE teachers, and 3) the assumption that all students in a class will be working on exactly the same materials and tasks at the same time.

Before addressing these specific points, it is important to note an age-old reality that predates OBE by centuries. It is the universal dilemma of managing the different learning rates and learning levels of students placed in the same classroom. One-room schoolhouse teachers faced it and handled it one way a century ago, often using the very same flexible-grouping, continuous progress, and learning team strategies being introduced in many OBE schools today. But the nature of the assembly-line delivery structure has encouraged an "everyone do everything at the same time" approach, which seriously limits the options available to teachers in self-contained/self-constrained, age-graded classrooms.

In fact, a variety of research findings indicate today's typical teacher has established an instructional pace consistent with about the 40th percentile of the class he or she is teaching. This means at least half of the class could go faster than the teacher is going.

Critics concerned that OBE instruction will force the faster students to "waste their time waiting" for the slower students to catch up need to be reminded of two things. One is that the typical classroom already exemplifies this problem. At least half of today's students already are waiting! The challenge is to introduce classroom methods that help teachers break this traditional lock-step pattern of delivery — which is clearly what more advanced forms of OBE do.

The second reminder is that this problem is tied to two particular practices found in some traditional Mastery Learning classrooms. First, teachers have students who don't do very well on an initial performance demonstration go through some type of "corrective loop" to improve their performance. The second practice relates to the techniques used to help these slower learners "catch up" with the learning challenges being pursued by the class as a whole. Critics assume that students who are successful on the initial performance will have to wait for other students to catch up or spend all of their time helping them do so — especially when cooperative learning is introduced into the situation. While these are legitimate concerns about classrooms in general, they can easily be avoided in all types of OBE models.

Avoiding the catch-up myth

First, even in fairly traditional versions of the Mastery Learning model, teachers are encouraged to avoid this potential "waiting" problem by having faster learners engage in challenging extension and enrichment activities once they have accomplished their basic work. Students pursue related content and concepts in-depth through stimulating projects and exercises while their classmates spend time mastering the initial material. This strategy gives focused attention to faster learners and continually provides them with opportunities to extend their learning without having to "wait" for slower learners to catch up. It is not, however, the same as employing an authentic continuous progress model that would allow them to move forward in the curriculum at their own pace whenever ready.

Second, those OBE practitioners who focus on developing more complex, life role outcomes (at the higher levels of the Demonstration Mountain shown in Figure 3.5) have an easier time avoiding this dilemma than do those focused on structured tasks and discrete content skills (the bottom of the Mountain). The former make deliberate attempts to create active learning communities in their classrooms and promote student learning through a variety of challenging pursuits, often by using a learning team or project structure. This approach:

- Improves the attention and motivation of almost all students.

- Directly enhances the classroom learning climate.

- Enables groups of students to take on large, complex projects that individual students could not hope to accomplish on their own.

- Keeps more advanced learners continuously challenged.

Third, teachers who pursue "Top of the Mountain" outcomes apply OBE's expanded opportunity principle to more than micro-outcomes and micro-time frames. This encourages students to adopt a "continuous growth and improvement" orientation to learning and achievement, rather than a "finite task" approach. But they do NOT view or implement the concept of expanded opportunity as a license for students to do as little as possible on a time schedule set by the slowest and least motivated students. Why? Because expanded opportunity is always balanced by a high expectations approach to having students accomplish clearly defined and implemented performance standards.

The expanded opportunity principle offers teachers and students flexibility in organizing instructional delivery arrangements, curriculum, and schedules. It also encourages staff to view time and personnel as flexible resources to be used in the smartest ways possible, without rigid adherence to the inflexible Industrial Age assembly-line structures and constraints of the past century. However, those parents and educators who have a great need for highly structured delivery and opportunity structures and strategies should be given the option of having their children in that kind of model. Of course, more flexible alternatives also should be available for those who see their advantages and want to use them.

Fourth, team-focused work should not be viewed, represented, or implemented as an attempt to compel students to interact with others against their will or to spend all of their time tutoring others instead of doing their own work. Nor should it be seen as an attempt to lower the achievement of the highest performers on a team to that of the lowest performers. Application of either OBE or cooperative learning that may inadvertently do any of these things must be significantly revised. Team-based learning and performing parallels the realities of the adult world: Individuals must develop their own competence and apply it effectively in the context of the groups and organizations in which they work and function. Neither the philosophies nor strategies that embody OBE or cooperative learning encourage students to abdicate personal responsibility for what they individually learn and contribute.

15. What groups have actively supported outcome-based reforms?

Support has come from three groups. The first comprises organizations that have actively been involved in shaping and promoting educational reforms and reform policies at state and national levels. Business groups at the state and local levels, the National Business Roundtable, the National Center for Education and the Economy, the National Governors' Association, and state legislatures and boards of education from coast to coast have all been openly supportive of, and have directly tried to shape and implement, the program alignment and external accountability approaches to OBE.

The second group includes organizations that have formally endorsed the purposes, philosophy, and principles of OBE without having directly supported its implementation. The 180,000-member Association for Supervision and Curriculum Development falls into this category.

The third group is made up of organizations that have actively disseminated accurate and positive information about OBE and have tried to counter the message and tactics of organized opposition groups. This third group includes the American Association of School Administrators, the Education Commission of the States, the Institute for Educational Leadership, the National Alliance for Business, the National Association of Secondary School Principals, the National Congress of Parents and Teachers, the National Education Association, the National Middle Schools Association, the National School Boards Association, and the National School Public Relations Association.

16. What do these advocacy and professional groups hope to gain through OBE implementation?

While some of these groups have not been closely politically aligned in the past, they do appear to have a common stake in the sound design and successful implementation of OBE because they share a commitment to building:

1) A significantly stronger public education system in the United States.

2) A more enlightened and competent citizenry capable of sustaining the nation's democratic processes and economic well-being.

OBE represents a powerful vehicle for helping change our educational system and expand the learning potential, opportunities, and success of all learners — a goal shared by all of these supportive organizations.

17. What other major school reform initiatives are closely allied with OBE?

Over the past two decades, OBE's "success for all" philosophy, focus on outcomes of significance, and emphasis on expanding opportunities and restructuring delivery and credentialing systems has allied it in people's minds and in practice with several kinds of educational reform efforts. The most obvious are the Mastery Learning work of Benjamin Bloom and James Block, the Effective Schools initiatives of Ronald Edmonds and Lawrence Lezotte, the Coalition of Essential Schools and Re-Learning work of Theodore Sizer, the New Standards Project of Lauren Resnick and her colleagues, and a host of other endeavors related to restructuring schools, curriculum integration, authentic assessment, site-based management, strategic planning, year-round schooling, and the quality movement.

In addition to all of these, the OBE critics identify it with many other visible components of current local school reform efforts, even though many of them have no direct relation to OBE at all. These other reforms also are being scrutinized, in their own right and as parts of the total OBE umbrella.

18. Are the controversies over all of these reforms reconcilable?

The differences in values, world views, and cause-effect perspectives between the advocates and critics of educational reforms seem great. On the surface, it appears few reasonable accommodations can be made. But individuals and organizations are working to transform existing battlegrounds into the common ground on which a larger reconciliation of views might be built. Their efforts have been bolstered by comments from leading critic Robert Simonds of Citizens for Excellence in Education. Simonds has stated publicly that his problem is not with outcomes, the principles of OBE, nor its more traditional applications, but with some of its more "non-academic transformational aspects that leave parents out of the picture" — definitely a piece of solid ground to build on.

Of the nine major issues just reviewed, it is likely that establishing common ground on five of the nine could reduce a great deal of the emotional controversy: the nature of outcomes, what OBE is, governmental control and accountability, cost versus effectiveness, and standards versus success. Reasoned discussion around just these five issues could go a long way toward defusing the unproductive and divisive "cluster argument" that characterizes OBE as a governmental plot to impose expensive and ineffective New Age ideas and values on students. Anything that can be done to reduce the credibility, currency, and visibility of this widespread misrepresentation of OBE will do more to enhance common understanding about outcome-based reforms than any other single action.

Summary

What are the most important things to remember about the opposition to OBE? Late in 1992, organized opposition to OBE effectively used the print and broadcast media to take its representations and interpretations of OBE to the public. Not until early 1994 did the picture begin to rebalance itself, as more and more broadcasters and reporters began to probe into OBE history, theory, and implementation. Many discovered that critics misunderstood the authentic essence and history of OBE and were consistently presenting a very distorted picture of it. The controversy surrounding OBE, then, was shaped by opposition characterized in these ways:

1) Most organized and vocal criticism against OBE was coming from one extreme end of the political spectrum.

2) The critics' tight political organization and the intense pressure it generated made the size, strength, and veracity of the opposition look greater than it was.

3) Several of the apparent motives that undergird this highly organized opposition extended well beyond either state or local educational issues or practices.

4) The opposition's arguments about what they labeled OBE often included things that had no direct or even indirect connection to OBE itself. Over time this "guilt by association" line of argument against OBE lost credibility.

The fact is, there are sound arguments in favor of OBE that directly counter each of the major issues of contention raised by the opposition. The more visibility these arguments and their accompanying evidence got, the less factual or emotional appeal the opposition's positions had and the less persuasive they became.

Chapter 7
Where Does OBE Go from Here?

Without question, Outcome-Based Education has become the educational reform
phenomenon of the '90s. As noted in Chapter
2, several compelling reasons explain its emer-
gence as a template to redirect, redefine, and
restructure the outdated features of our time-
based, Industrial Age system of public education. Consequently, it is clearly worth explor-
ing how the history of outcome-based thinking and practice is likely to unfold.

1. Where does OBE go from here?

This speculative question will be easier to answer if we can put some specifics
or conditions around both it and its answers. One set of conditions is the
timeline to which the question applies. The potential scenario of the middle
'90s is likely to differ from that of the late '90s and beyond, so the answers will
reflect that difference. Another condition has to do with the overall scope and
depth of implementation that may occur, so the answers reflect variations
along that dimension as well. Finally, the nature of the implementation itself
is a critical factor in shaping any future scenarios, so the answers will strongly
focus on the diverse possibilities related to this third dimension.

Let's start with the near future and then develop some longer term scenarios from there. From all appearances, at least six conditions are bound to determine the course of OBE policy and implementation over the next few years:

1) Outcome-based or performance-based approaches are inherently part of a larger societal shift to the Information Age taking place around us. Those larger changes and shifts will not be reversed by political reactions to specific education policies or reform efforts. This implies that the greater societal pressures both for specific kinds of outcomes and for overall system reform will not abate.

2) The commonsense nature of outcome-based models, as well as the successes of districts and schools that have taken care to implement OBE well, establish an aura of credibility around OBE. Inevitably, this view will prevail in the midst of heated political debates currently taking place at all political and institutional levels.

3) The many national organizations and bodies that have declared themselves in favor of either OBE specifically or of progressive education reforms in general will combine forces and begin to campaign actively and politically to ensure needed reforms are not scuttled.

4) The tremendous diversity of practices called OBE will continue to fuel both the pro and con political forces currently in play. The weaknesses of several of the current state models will diminish the quality of longer range OBE implementation prospects, since they are bound to affect the direction and impetus of what happens in their states for years to come. OBE opponents will, therefore, be able to continue to attack the visible shortcomings of what they currently represent as OBE.

5) Positive dialogue has begun between key OBE leaders and those representing some of the opposition groups identified in Chapter 6. These dialogues are likely to establish areas of agreement about OBE and its defining elements, and to

reduce some of the strident emotionalism surrounding most OBE criticism. The most likely outcome of these ongoing discussions will be strong endorsement for what amounts to "OBE Alternatives" — multiple models of OBE co-existing at the local level, including a "traditionalist" alternative that the opposition groups find acceptable and endorse.

6) Despite the progress that may be forthcoming from discussions between OBE advocacy and opposition groups, many OBE opponents will not back off their goal of derailing either OBE itself or any other attempts to fundamentally strengthen and restructure the system of public education in the United States — especially attempts emanating from the federal government. The reasons are tied to other issues that simply have made OBE a convenient target for the larger ultra-conservative national political agenda.

The short-term future of OBE

With these and other forces operating simultaneously at local, state, and national levels, the following six principles are likely to characterize the short-term future of OBE.

1) Recognize that some aspects and versions of OBE will be more politically acceptable in certain communities than in others. Those who favor OBE will go out of their way to clearly define and describe all of the essential components and alternative modes of implementation inherent in OBE systems.

A key part of this message will be that states and districts have clear alternatives to choose from in terms of the outcomes they pursue and the way they organize and structure themselves to achieve them. Knowing what these alternatives and their components and likely implications are will greatly assist potential implementers in developing and offering to their clientele the range of models best suited for their communities. In addition, advocates will use a variety of channels and strategies for communicating this multiple-models message to the public.

2) Specify key types of outcomes. OBE advocates will more clearly identify specific kinds of outcomes and outcome frameworks available to states and districts than has been done to date. Specifically, efforts will be made to emphasize and distinguish among literacy outcomes that underlie all other learning; curriculum outcomes that establish the content that students will learn in the curriculum; and performance outcomes that use literacy and curriculum in applications of learning that tie more directly to real-life challenges and responsibilities.

3) Establish local alternative models of OBE. Diverse outcome frameworks and multiple implementation possibilities will be combined and explained to districts as available alternatives. From these choices, districts can build or choose any set of combinations that meet the needs of their community and state. Given the current state of affairs in the field, three major configurations are likely to emerge as alternatives from which policymakers, parents, and educators can choose. They include:

- A traditional structure model that uses literacy outcomes and curriculum outcomes as its culminating expectations for students, focuses on the lower sectors of the Demonstration Mountain, and organizes curriculum, instruction, assessment, and reporting accordingly. This would be similar to many of the early program alignment models of OBE (described in Figure 4.2 in Chapter 4) and would retain many of the age-graded, self-contained classroom program and organizational structures of schools so familiar to parents. A variation on this model might include a curriculum emphasis congenial to many of the current OBE opposition groups. Except for consistently applying OBE's four principles in individual classrooms, this model would strongly resemble the traditional schools of this century.

- A flexible structure model that uses literacy outcomes and curriculum outcomes as enabling components for a broad range of interdisciplinary, higher order performance outcomes focused on the middle and upper levels of the Demonstration Mountain. Curriculum, instruction, assessment, and reporting would take on a decidedly authentic performance/interdisciplinary/flexible grouping and scheduling/teacher teaming character. This model would integrate features of the more advanced applications of the program alignment approach (described in Chapter 4, Figure 4.2) and some aspects of the system transformation approach (described in Figure 4.4).

- A future applications model that also uses literacy outcomes and curriculum outcomes as enabling components for a comprehensive set of challenging, role-performance outcomes (including the life performance framework described in Figure 3.6 of Chapter 3). This model would embody most of the features of the system transformation approach described in Figure 4.4, including its emphasis on 1) developing and applying future-focused complex role performance abilities in real-world learning and performance settings with extensive use of outside experts as program designers and instructors; 2) pursuing a strong issue-driven interdisciplinary curriculum; 3) developing a range of authentic and alternative assessment and record-keeping tools; and 4) operating an open-access/multiple technologies instructional system that operates year-round with extended days and weeks. It would inherently encourage continual innovation of technology, curriculum, instructional, assessment, and reporting systems that directly support and reflect these high-level, future-focused performance abilities.

Given the realities surrounding reform initiatives of all kinds today, it seems probable that communities are most likely to include the traditional structure model in any initial OBE efforts with the expectation of adding, or evolving to, viable examples of the flexible structure model as well. Ongoing tech-prep models and current school-to-work initiatives promoted by the federal government will provide districts with incentives to choose the future applications model, even though it is unfamiliar and its implementation involves innovative practices.

4) Develop sound assessments. Pro-OBE groups, along with some opposition groups, will insist that sound assessments be developed for any outcome performance that has a major bearing on a student's status within the system. This pertains to grades earned, promotion, program placement, and graduation. The transition period needed to adequately define, design, and develop these measures is bound to be chaotic since assessment and evaluation policies and practices are among the most emotionally and politically charged issues in all of education. The success of OBE in the longer run will hinge directly on how well both the defining and assessing of outcomes is done during this critical transition period.

5) Press for new university admissions criteria. At the same time, these pro-OBE groups will continue to press for changes in criteria and procedures that govern admissions to colleges and universities to make them more consistent with the outcomes being pursued within each state. This is bound to be easier for implementers of the traditional structure model of OBE; stimulate closer connections between higher education and K-12 reform policies; and have an impact on both instructional and credentialing practices within the higher education system itself. Oregon is the leading example of these particular changes to date, but several other states and Canadian provinces already have begun serious discussions about modifying existing criteria.

6) Anticipate continued challenges. Despite the existence of the traditional structure alternative, some of the most nationally organized opposition groups will continue to vigorously challenge OBE. This will keep some local districts under political pressure, sustain the climate of intimidation that many of them currently face, and decrease the chance in the long run of some of them making any real advances with OBE in the short run.

2. What is the most optimistic scenario of the future of outcome-based reforms?

The best-case scenario of OBE's future emanates directly from a combination of the first three and the fifth conditions noted at the beginning of the chapter. These conditions will give great impetus to the mid-'90s scenarios just described.

The essence of this good news picture in the longer run is that most states will have revisited and revised their original reform policies and traditional credentialing systems to encourage and support their local districts in implementing the strongest features of the three OBE models. Among the most important state actions are:

1) The elimination of Carnegie unit course credits as the basis for defining and determining student graduation from high school.

2) The establishment of a variety of citizen/educator task forces charged with continuously monitoring changes in future trends and recommending to all local districts updates in outcome frameworks.

3) The establishment of a variety of distance learning options and delivery systems for students desiring specialized assistance in learning areas not available locally.

4) The establishment of research and development centers within the states focused on the continuous improvement of instructional and assessment methods geared to all three kinds of outcome frameworks that parents and school district staff are free to attend to upgrade their skills in working with students.

These state initiatives will be paralleled by two key stakeholder institutions and consumers: each state's higher education system and its key employer groups. Working together with task forces of educators, experts, and citizens, both groups will develop a common template of literacy outcomes, curriculum outcomes, and higher level performance outcomes, supplemented by evidence of relevant prior experiences, that both institutions will regularly use in their respective admissions and employment screening processes.

In addition, the higher education systems of these states will initiate three significant internal changes to support OBE implementation: 1) the development of learner outcome frameworks for all on-campus and extension courses offered under their jurisdiction; 2) the establishment of OBE-grounded programs for the preparation of administrators and teachers going into the field of education; and 3) a program of visiting scholars to work directly with local districts and their students on major developments in their fields.

Likewise, the business community will establish collaborative arrangements with consortia of local districts whereby students can receive varying amounts of direct work-site experience in a variety of fields to supplement their in-school learning experiences, and local experts can work directly with students and staff in support of both pertinent curriculum outcomes and high-level performance outcomes.

These state, higher education, and employer initiatives will be directly mirrored in the widespread implementation of all three OBE models by the majority of local districts and private schools in those states and by the heavy involvement of parents, community members, and local experts in their ongoing implementation and refinement. Among the most conspicuous changes in local districts will be:

- The availability and continuing refinement of three different kinds of OBE models for parents and students to choose from, each focused on a key set of literacy, curriculum, and performance outcomes that articulate with higher education and workplace entrance standards.

- Heavy local participation in each model, focused on monitoring changes in future trends, and assisting in instructional delivery and the assessment of key outcomes.

- Clear expectations that all students have timely access to the learning experiences and instructional supports that directly facilitate their accomplishment of the district's key literacy, curriculum, and performance outcomes.

- All programs and learning experiences directly tied to, and organized around, what the district has defined as its key literacy, curriculum, and performance outcomes for all its students.

- College-level learning experiences available to students on an on-demand basis through distance learning and other high-technology delivery options.

This widespread OBE implementation will be made possible through determined efforts of many national organizations and their local affiliates, all conducting information campaigns within their states and communities during the mid-'90s. They will clearly define the principles and purposes of OBE; describe essential literacy, curriculum, and performance outcomes needed for student success both in and beyond school; advocate the implementation of alternative approaches to OBE at the local level; and take their case directly to the press and to the public, asking for their input and involvement as alternative models take shape.

The national associations' work will parallel that of OBE advocates and implementers who establish a continuing dialogue with former critics of outcome-based reforms at the state and local levels. These dialogues will be crucial to changing OBE opposition into understanding of potential benefits for all its students and their families and to successfully implementing OBE in public and private schools.

3. What is the least optimistic scenario of the future of outcome-based reforms in the late '90s and beyond?

If the dialogue and interventions described in the previous paragraph do not take place, it is possible to imagine a discouraging political and practical future for all forms of progressive educational reform. To remain a strong reform alternative, OBE will need the committed and sustained support of the many institutions described as its supporters in Chapter 6. This support is essential to the volume and quality of press and visibility OBE will need to counteract the extensive coverage its critics received during the early '90s. If the current intensity of outspoken opposition and political action against OBE and related reforms at the local and state levels continues unabated, and if opposition candidates get elected to local school boards in large numbers, local communities could face a variety of narrow interest programmatic and policy changes being introduced into their schools. And, as happened in some districts in the early '90s, the threat to remove key staff who represent or advocate other views will become very real.

Consequently, in the mid-'90s, opportunities for establishing a potential common ground with key opposition leaders and groups are critical. Without them, the verbal and political attacks some local educators currently are experiencing will continue to discourage them from pursuing anything that does not conform with the critics' views of education.

Should this negative set of conditions come to pass, public educators may face a future in which either advocating or implementing OBE will guarantee a strong reaction and pressure from the critics until OBE is either diluted significantly or forced underground. By default, that is likely to leave the time-based, Industrial Age paradigm of schooling intact, academic programs and tracks as widely separated from technical programs as ever, and public schools less and less able to respond to society's demands for change and improvement.

In addition, this worst-case scenario portends a widening cultural and political polarization in society in which a relatively small, well-financed and organized minority would be able to stalemate educational reform by preventing others from exercising their preferences. With reform stalemated, public schools would find it difficult to improve. Failure rates and dropout rates would continue to increase for those segments of the population currently labeled "at risk," and schools would remain open to charges of ineffectiveness and the need for vouchers and private alternatives.

The latter, in turn, opens the door for a major redefinition of the private school education system, which many fear will undermine society's ability to establish a common core of civic values to nurture healthy democratic institutions. Some speculate that increases in socioeconomic, racial, cultural, and educational separatism would occur, and the common ground for children of diverse backgrounds to learn and work side by side with each other would begin to disappear. With opportunities for interracial and intercultural opportunities minimized, a society that is becoming more diverse may further fragment itself into separate educational, economic, and cultural enclaves.

4. What is the most probable scenario for the future of outcome-based reforms in the late '90s and beyond?

Two key factors are so predominant in shaping the scenarios of OBE's longer term future that a "most probable" scenario is not hard to develop. As described at the outset of this chapter, the first factor is the massive impetus for change sweeping the economic and political systems of society.

These change forces will continue to press for clearer and better educational results and for delivery systems that guarantee and document student learning success, a huge plus for OBE.

The second factor is the broad diversity of OBE initiatives already underway in states and districts. While weaknesses in some of those efforts provide continuing fuel for critics, these OBE initiatives offer a fertile ground for growing and refining at least the three models identified earlier in the chapter. Support for these reforms ranges from lukewarm to scalding hot, and is likely to be sustained and strengthened as more and more press coverage and professional information reaches educators and the public about:

- Ways many of these existing efforts can and should be improved to take advantage of the power inherent in OBE's purposes, principles, and operating paradigm.

- Ways parents and the public can productively be involved in shaping and strengthening these models.

Given that these two messages can be disseminated broadly and convincingly, the most likely future of OBE is that it will both survive the '90s and become the new paradigm around which public and private schools and public and private higher education can focus. This will require extensive commitment from historical supporters of OBE and the willing participation of some of those initial opponents who come to see, through the search for a common ground, how OBE can work to their direct advantage.

An unfolding story. The most probable scenario, then, is that the paradigm shift toward an outcome-based, Information Age system of education will continue — sporadically at first because of all of the negatives in the current picture and the distrust of various state and federal initiatives — but becoming increasingly more positive as the decade progresses. This progress ultimately will institutionalize a variety of implementation models including the three identified earlier in the chapter as well as their inevitable hybrids. A prudent guess is that the short-term preference for the traditional structure model will eventually evolve into a strong preference for the flexible structure model as it becomes more familiar and proves itself through meaningful results.

The last to receive widespread public endorsement will be the future applications model — simply because it is unfamiliar and needs to evolve — but it is bound to ride the wave of Information Age change and is likely to emerge eventually as the model for the year 2000 and beyond.

5. What can those who support outcome-based reforms do to keep them alive in their districts and states?

The opposition to OBE during the early '90s has been seriously distracting to those committed to its implementation. Consequently, those who see the merit in what has been described in this book should recognize from the outset that support for OBE may, in the eyes of some, look controversial. Therefore, those who choose to actively support OBE reform efforts in their district or state should include the following in their plans:

- Prepare! Become thoroughly familiar with the issues and content in all seven chapters of this book. Read them again and again so that both the substance and the frameworks behind the substance are clear and can be comfortably and simply communicated to others. Remember that the opposition already has saturated the public and press with its definitions and views. OBE advocates will have to be very well prepared in order to deal with the many impressions people have. Share the book with anyone interested in these issues — pro and con.

- Prepare even more! Read the March 1994 issue of *Educational Leadership* and the September 1994 issue of the *School Administrator* thoroughly and notice the differences in definitions, terms, and examples used. Learn to live with these inconsistencies while developing your own consistent definitions. Also, study the policies being proposed by your state and your district. Be prepared to compare them directly with what you have read and studied about OBE. Often, those policies or proposals will differ from what you have learned. Be prepared to describe those differences.

- Contact your state administrator and school boards associations. Find out what their plans and strategies are for supporting outcome-based reforms and volunteer to support their efforts. The same is true, of course, with your local school district and PTA. Offer to participate in meetings and forums on these issues. If none is planned, help plan some. Be sure that everyone possible has read some of the important work on OBE — especially your local school board members. If community members base what they know about OBE on what they've heard on certain radio call-in shows, it's likely to be a very distorted picture. Help inform them ahead of time.

- Go out of your way to share what you know about OBE and school reform issues with people in the community. The most informal occasions are often the best for finding people open to consider these issues. Keep the dialogue positive and focus on facts, not opinions and innuendo. Ask businesspeople, clergy, and other community leaders to do the same. They all have a lot to lose and gain from how these educational reform initiatives are defined and carried out. Most of them are key opinion leaders. Go out of your way to give them sound, honest information and perspectives.

- Be willing to seek outside expertise. This pertains to the technical design side of OBE and to dealing with the opposition. Most of the examples of "OBE" that critics ridicule are hindered by inadequate technical support. In some cases, state and local implementation is in jeopardy because of shortcomings that could have been avoided.

- Encourage open, fair public discussions and debates about all education reform issues. Insist on democratic, highly participatory decision making when it directly affects policies and programs. Framing issues as all black/all white unnecessarily polarizes them and inevitably leaves communities divided. Encourage policymakers to offer options and alternatives on seriously controversial issues, rather than win/lose, in/out consequences.

- Introduce and implement reforms at a pace both the education staff and the community can support. Patience taken at the beginning is the best guarantee of minimizing grief at the latter stages of implementation. Districts that have taken the time to heavily involve and educate their staff and communities have reaped the benefits of strong public support when faced with opposition groups.

6. What are the most important things to remember about where OBE goes from here?

The major impetus for current outcome-based reforms coast to coast is a matter of both institutional urgency and individual common sense. People want it, and the schools need it. Consequently, OBE seems destined to have a viable future as long as open democratic processes prevail in our society, and strong professional norms continue to govern the field of education.

Conclusion

Those who would eagerly embrace or decry OBE as a major force in shaping the future of education in North America should frequently revisit its paradigm, purposes, premises, and principles described in Chapter 1. For that is where OBE either meets or fails the test of public scrutiny and professional integrity. WHAT and WHETHER are more important than WHEN and HOW in designing and operating learning systems. Either OBE's purposes speak to the challenges of our times and aspirations of our citizens, or they don't. Either its premises reflect a deeply felt, realistic optimism about the inherent potential of humans to learn and succeed, or they don't. Either its principles pave the way for successful learning designs and experiences for all learners, or they don't.

Yes, all the rest is simply details! But it's up to each one of us to be sure the details of policy and daily practice do justice to the foundation set by true OBE principles and components intended to improve children's education now and for the future.

Glossary

Assessment: Generic term for the process of gathering information on the quality of a product, performance, or demonstration. Assessment typically implies the use of methods other than traditional paper and pencil testing.

Authentic Assessment: The process of gathering information directly pertinent to the quality of a performance that "perfectly embodies" all of the defined aspects of the performance — hence the term "authentic."

Civic Values: Values widely shared by members of a community or society, which make civilized living possible. Honesty and respect for others' property are typical examples.

Content Outcomes: Demonstrations of learning in which a command of specific content is more important than the processes that might be used to demonstrate that command.

Context: The physical setting or situation in which a learning demonstration takes place.

Criterion: An essential performance component used to judge its completeness and quality.

Criterion-Based: A system in which clearly defined criteria are the basis for organizing actions and making decisions.

Culminating Outcomes: Demonstrations of learning that occur at or after the end of formal learning experiences. The term sometimes is used synonymously with the term exit outcomes.

Design Down: One of the key principles of an outcome-based system, in which curriculum planning starts with the intended outcome and proceeds back to an instructional starting point.

Discrete Outcomes: Usually small, highly specific learning demonstrations that stand alone and have little direct bearing on the learning of other outcomes.

Enabling Outcomes: Learning demonstrations that are essential building blocks for learning other more complex outcomes.

Exit Outcomes: Learning demonstrations that define the system's ultimate expectations for students, occurring at or after the end of students' school careers.

Hierarchy: A framework of ranking the superordinate and subordinate relationships among system elements.

Higher Order Competencies: A broad group of demonstrable processes requiring the complex manipulation of information, concepts, and language. Typical examples include problem solving, critical thinking, decision making, and communication.

Inclusionary Success: A key attribute of an outcome-based system, denoting the commitment to implement conditions that enable success for as many learners and staff as possible.

Life Role: A set of responsibilities and actions that define an individual's position within a society's economic, political, and social relationships. Being a citizen, employer, employee, parent, and family member are typical examples.

Literacy Outcomes: Demonstrations of learning that pertain directly to competence in reading, writing, speaking, listening, and computation.

Operational Structures: Key patterns of action and decision making in an organization that govern what, how, and when things get done. In schools, these structures include how performance standards, curriculum, instruction, and grouping are defined and carried out.

Outcome-Based Education: A comprehensive approach to organizing and operating an education system that is focused on and defined by the successful demonstrations of learning sought from each student.

Outcomes: Learning results that are clearly demonstrated at or after the end of an instructional experience. Outcomes can take many forms (from simple to complex) depending on the content, competencies, performance contexts, and consequences embodied in their definition.

Outcomes of Significance: Demonstrations of learning that have major consequences for one's later learning and living.

Performance Credentialing: Awarding certificates, diplomas, degrees, or other symbols of qualification or accomplishment based on the demonstration of clearly defined competencies.

Performance Outcomes: Demonstrations of learning in which command of clearly identified competencies and performance abilities is the central factor to accomplishment.

Performance Role: A set of responsibilities and actions that constitute a key part of most life roles. Typical examples include learner, communicator, problem solver, and producer.

Performance Standards: The standards and criteria by which a performance's completeness and quality is judged.

Personal Values: The values held by individuals in a society that shape their personal goals, beliefs, choices, orientations, and actions.

Role: A set of responsibilities and actions that define an individual's position and expected behavior within a given social system.

Role Performance: A demonstration of the competencies and abilities required in carrying out the responsibilities and actions of a role or position within a social system.

Rubric: A framework of criteria used to define and assess the essential attributes of a performance.

Stakeholder: An individual or group with a direct interest in the functioning, effectiveness, or success of an organization. In education, the term typically refers to parents, educators, students, taxpayers, and a variety of community groups.

Standard: The set of qualities or measures by which performance, skills, or other types of knowledge is judged. These measures can vary along a set of dimensions, including objective-subjective, absolute-relative, substantive-comparative.

Strategic Design: A systematic process for determining a district's key directions and for deriving its mission, framework of exit outcomes, and operating priorities. The process involves careful analysis of information pertaining to future trends and conditions.

Strategic Planning: A systematic process for determining a district's mission and priorities, as well as its action plans and responsibilities for carrying them out.

Time-Based: A comprehensive approach to organizing and operating a system in which the clock and calendar determine actions and decision making.

Traditional: A term used to describe educational planning and implementation based on subject matter categories and organizational arrangements that have characterized education systems for the past century. The term "disciplinary" refers to this approach.

Transformational: A term used to describe educational planning and implementation emanating from careful examination of life's dimensions and conditions. This information redefines and restructures traditional education structures and processes that are incompatible with those conditions.

Transitional: A term used to describe educational planning and implementation that focuses on higher order competencies and their role in connecting and potentially integrating unconnected, content-focused curriculum areas. The term interdisciplinary characterizes this approach.

Bibliography

Barker, Joel. *Discovering the Future: The Business of Paradigms*. Burnsville, Minn.: ChartHouse International, 1990.

Block, James H. *Mastery Learning: Theory and Practice*. New York: Holt, Rinehart, and Winston, 1971.

Block, James H., Helen Efthim, and Robert Burns. *Building Effective Mastery Learning Schools*. White Plains: Longman, 1989.

Bloom, Benjamin S. "Learning for Mastery," UCLA Evaluation Comment, 1(2), 1-12, 1968.

Burron, Arnold. "Traditionalist Christians and OBE: What's the Problem?" *Educational Leadership*, (1994) 51(6), 73-75.

Covey, Stephen R. *Principle Centered Leadership.*, New York: Summit Books, 1991.

Covey, Stephen R. *The Seven Habits of Highly Effective People: Restoring the Character Ethic*. New York: Simon and Schuster, 1989.

Gardner, Howard. *Frames of Mind: The Theory of Multiple Intelligence.* New York,: Basic Books, 1985.

Gardner, Howard. *Multiple Intelligences: The Theory in Practice.* New York: Basic Books, 1993.

Hammer, Michael and James Champy. *Reengineering the Corporation: A Manifesto for Business.* New York: Harper Business, 1993.

Kuhn, Thomas S. *The Structure of Scientific Revolutions.* Chicago: University of Chicago Press, 1970.

Marzanno, Robert J. "When Two Worldviews Collide," (1993) *Educational Leadership,* 51(4), 6-11.

Peters, Thomas and Robert Waterman. *In Search of Excellence.* New York: Harper and Row, 1982.

Report of the Secretary's Commission on Achieving Needed Goals. Washington, D.C.: U.S. Department of Labor, 1992.

Senge, Peter M. *The Fifth Discipline: The Art and Practice of the Learning Organization.* New York: Doubleday/Currency, 1990.

Simonds, Robert. "A Plea for the Children," *Educational Leadership,* (1993) 51(4), 12-15.

Sizer, Theodore R. "High School Reform: The Need for Engineering," (June, 1993) *Kappan,* 64, 679-683.

Sizer, Theodore R. *Horace's Compromise: The Dilemma of the American High School.* Boston: Houghton Mifflin, 1984.

Toffler, Alvin. *Powershift: Knowledge, Wealth, and Violence at the Edge of the 21st Century.* New York: Bantam, 1990.

OBE Implementation Resources

The following organizations provide direct OBE implementation assistance of various kinds to school districts and schools throughout North America.

CENTER FOR OUTCOME-BASED EDUCATION

Alan Cohen, Director
University of San Francisco
2130 Fulton Street
San Francisco, CA 94117-1080
Phone: (415) 666-2102

HIGH SUCCESS NETWORK

William Spady, Director
P.O. Box 1630
Eagle, CO 81631-1630
Phone: (303) 328-1688

NATIONAL CENTER
FOR OUTCOME-BASED EDUCATION
John Champlin, Director
10115 E. Bella Vista
Scottsdale, AZ 85258
Phone: (602) 661-0495

NETWORK FOR OUTCOME-BASED SCHOOLS
William Smith, Director
6 Marydale
Brookhaven, NY 11719
Phone: (516) 286-0705

OUTCOMES ASSOCIATES
Charlotte Danielson, President
P.O. Box 7285
Princeton, NJ 08543-7285
Phone: (609) 683-0955

PARTNERS FOR QUALITY LEARNING
Albert Mamary, Director
P.O. Box 185
Syracuse, NY 13211
Phone: (800) 5JOINUS

Background Reading on OBE

Readers wishing to learn more about the background and history of OBE are encouraged to pursue the following publications and articles.

James H. Block (ed.). *Schools, Society, and Mastery Learning.* (New York: Holt, Rinehart, and Winston, 1974).

John B. Carroll, (1963) "A Model of School Learning," *Teachers College Record,* 64 (December) 723-733.

Educational Leadership, (1994) 51(6), entire issue.

I. Lee Gray and Glenn M. Hymel (eds.). *Successful Schooling for All: A Primer on Outcome-Based Education and Mastery Learning.* (Johnson City, New York: Network for Outcome-Based Schools, 1992).

Daniel U. Levine and associates (eds.). *Improving Student Achievement Through Mastery Learning.* (San Francisco: Jossy-Bass, 1985).

Douglas E. Mitchell and William G. Spady, (1978) "Organizational Contexts for Implementing Outcome-Based Education," *Educational Researcher,* 7(7), 9-17.

Outcomes, the quarterly publication of the Network for Outcome-Based Schools since 1980.

Stephen E. Rubin and William G. Spady, (1984) "Achieving Excellence Through Outcome-Based Instructional Delivery," *Educational Leadership,* 41(8), 37-44.

William G. Spady, (1977) "Competency-Based Education: A Bandwagon in Search of a Definition," *Educational Researcher,* 6(1), 9-14.

_____, (1978) "The Concept and Implications of Competency-Based Education," *Educational Leadership,* 36 (October), 16-22.

_____, (1982) "Outcome-Based Instructional Management: Its Sociological Implications," *Australian Journal of Education,* 26(2), 123-143.

_____, (1986) "The Emerging Paradigm of Organizational Excellence: Success through Planned Adaptability," *Peabody Journal of Education,* 63(3), 46-63.

_____, (1987) "On Grades, Grading, and School Reform," *Outcomes,* 6(1), 7-12.

_____, (1987) "Outcome-Based Implementation in High Schools: Things We Are Learning," *Outcomes,* 6(4), 1-8.

_____, (1988) "Organizing for Results: The Basis of Authentic Restructuring and Reform," *Educational Leadership,* 46(2), 4-10.

_____, (1991) "Shifting the Grading Paradigm That Pervades Education," *Outcomes,* 9(4), 39-45.

_____, (1992) "It's Time To Take a Close Look at Outcome-Based Education" *Outcomes*, 11(2), 6-13.

_____, (1994) "Choosing Outcomes of Significance," *Educational Leadership*, 51(6), 18-22.

_____, (1994) "What's All the Talk About Outcome-Based Education?" *PTA Today*, 19(5), 17-18.

William G. Spady and Kit J. Marshall, (1991) "Beyond Traditional Outcome-Based Education," *Educational Leadership*, 49(2), 67-72.

William G. Spady and Douglas E. Mitchell, (1977) "Competency-Based Education: Organizational Issues and Implications," *Educational Researcher*, 6(2), 9-15.

Acknowledgments

This book is the result of 25 years of persistent inquiry into the meaning, implications, and applications of what we know today as Outcome-Based Education. Its power and potential are compelling enough to keep me engaged for another 25 years, but this is the snapshot of where OBE stands in mid-1994. Like all important concepts, OBE has gone through several stages of evolution, and that evolution continues to this day. The term OBE has acquired many different usages and applications, and it has attracted a large number of advocates and its share of vocal critics. That helps explain why this book went through several writings and revisions, and why it should not be read or interpreted as the final word on the subject. OBE will continue to evolve.

OBE's fundamentals are simple, but they have profound implications for changing the most prevalent patterns of practice embedded in the educational systems of the 20th century. Its bases are pure common sense, but they open the door to complex issues for which conventional models of education have few answers. I suspect that readers who examine these issues carefully will be as compelled as I have been to find creative and useful ways for addressing them. That appears to be the constant challenge presented by new paradigms.

Many people have contributed directly to my career-long pursuit of these issues. John Carroll's insights of 30 years ago about schools, aptitude, time, and learning were the original catalyst. The ideas and work of Benjamin Bloom and James Block in the '70s were pivotal in my addressing the notions surrounding nontraditional models of curriculum, instruction, assessment, and credentialing. During the '70s and '80s, John Champlin and Albert Mamary's pioneering work in the Johnson City Central Schools proved that the ideas of these important scholars were both powerful and realistic. Alan Cohen, Joan Hyman, Stephen Rubin, and many others confirmed during the '70s and '80s that the OBE paradigm had extraordinary power.

The impetus, encouragement, and support for writing this book comes from many sources, all of whom believe deeply in OBE's power and potential. My colleagues in the High Success Network have put in many years developing, refining, and implementing all aspects of outcome-based designs and delivery systems, and each has contributed mightily to the frameworks presented here. John Artis, Helen Burz, Kit Marshall, Spence Rogers, Alan Rowe, and Chuck Schwahn all added significantly to the book's substance, and Marjorie Ledell and Raynette Sanchez provided valuable editorial comments throughout. My sister Sha Spady used her creativity and practicality to shape its structure and focus.

Special thanks go to AASA Senior Associate Executive Director Gary Marx, Publications Manager Leslie Eckard, and Communications Assistant Katie Ross of AASA for their exceptional confidence and support of this project. Their encouragement, understanding, patience, and editorial expertise and feedback kept this endeavor on track and brought it to fruition. Special thanks also go to Ron Brandt of ASCD for his support of this project and his ever-insightful contributions to its substance and dissemination to the field — and to Arnold Burron, Marshall Fritz, and Robert Simonds for generously leading their unique perspectives and deep personal support to critiques of these chapters. A special thank you also goes to Joel Klein who ably and cheerfully designed and refined each graphic until it met our needs.

Finally, my profoundest thanks go to the individuals mentioned in Chapter 5 — the practitioner champions of the OBE movement — plus countless other practitioners not mentioned. They have made OBE work, and without them OBE would be pure theory. These individuals and their colleagues deserve enormous credit from their fellow educators for having made change happen in the face of the enormous institutional inertia surrounding our education system. That is the ultimate test of leadership in our times, and they have passed it with flying colors.

—William Spady

About the Author

William G. Spady

William G. Spady is internationally recognized as one of the major theorists, writers, developers, and leaders in the Outcome-Based Education movement. He serves as director of the High Success Network in Eagle, Colorado, which he founded in 1986 as a vehicle for directly helping educators, policymakers, and communities implement the inherent power of OBE in their schools.

Spady is a native of Milwaukie, Oregon, and holds three degrees from the University of Chicago — in humanities, education, and sociology. Between 1967 and 1973 he held academic appointments in the Sociology of Education at Harvard University and the Ontario Institute for Studies in Education. His commitment to OBE began in earnest while a senior research sociologist at the National Institute of Education in 1973, and it expanded extensively during the '70s and '80s while he served as associate executive director of the American Association of School Administrators and as director of the Far West Laboratory for Educational Research and Development.

In 1980, Spady helped found the Network for Outcome-Based Schools, served as its executive director for five years, edited its quarterly publication, *Outcomes*, for six, and served on its board of directors for 12 years. His many articles and frameworks related to OBE have influenced its evolution and implementation internationally.